In Their Generations

Wega Miller George

Black Rose Writing
www.blackrosewriting.com

© 2011 by Wega Miller George

All rights reserved. No part of this book may be reproduced, stored in a retrieval system or transmitted in any form or by any means without the prior written permission of the publishers, except by a reviewer who may quote brief passages in a review to be printed in a newspaper, magazine or journal.

The final approval for this literary material is granted by the author.

First printing

All characters appearing in this work are real, as the author depicts the following as an informative memoir.

ISBN: 978-1-61296-049-4
PUBLISHED BY BLACK ROSE WRITING
www.blackrosewriting.com

Printed in the United States of America

In Their Generations is printed in Times New Roman

*Dedicated with love to my daughters,
Kathy and Taela,
And to the next generation, and the next...*

Let us now praise famous men,
And our fathers in their generations.

Ecclesiasticus 44:1

Introduction
by Richard Pankhurst

This remarkable history, based on letters and diaries, as well as many intimate memories of the family collected over the years, begins with John Bell (the great-great-grandfather of the author). Bell, though now largely forgotten, was in his day a significant figure in nineteenth century relations between Europe and Africa. A retired British naval officer, and sometime British consul in Aleppo, Syria, he conceived the idea – shared by not a few of his compatriots - of traveling to Ethiopia to visit the Source of the mighty River Nile. This was no easy task for the age-old Christian empire was then in the grips of civil war.

Bell later befriended another Englishman, Walter Plowden, and the two decided to spend their lives in Ethiopia. Both wore Ethiopian white cotton clothing, and learnt to speak Amharic. Plowden got himself appointed British Consul, and engineered the signing in 1849 of a Treaty between Britain and Ethiopia – one of the first ever concluded between Britain and an African state, while Bell attached himself to the Ethiopian court, received a prominent Ethiopian title, and married into the high Ethiopian aristocracy.

This was an important time in Ethiopian history, for it witnessed the rise of Emperor Tewodros (or Theodore), a reforming monarch – and would-be unifier of the country, who, having fought his way to power, won great admiration from both Plowden and Bell. The latter spent many hours telling Tewodros of the wonders of the Industrial Revolution in Europe – and reciting Shakespeare, but he and his friend Plowden were both soon afterwards killed while fighting against rebels in 1860.

~

Bell's involvement with Ethiopia did not however stop then – for at the time of his death he had three young children by his

Ethiopian wife…

Each one of them plays a significant role in Wega George's fascinating narrative…

Emperor Tewodros was then facing almost insuperable difficulties – with rebels rising against him in all directions, and his access to the coast blocked.

Several years earlier he had accepted an offer from Bishop Samuel Gobat, the renowned British ecclesiastic in Jerusalem, proposing to send him Protestant missionaries trained at the St. Chrischona missionary institute in Switzerland – who, while teaching the Bible, would also assist the reforming Ethiopian ruler in technical matters. These lay craftsmen-missionaries, overcoming considerable difficulties, made their way up the Nile to Ethiopia, where they were settled on a hill called Gaffat near Tewodros's capital. Two of them, Theophilus Waldmeier, a Swiss, and Karl Saalmüller, a German, married the two Bell daughters, Susan and Mary respectively – and were involved in the drama of building a massive mortar for Tewodros, which he named Sebastopol after one of the military engagements of the Crimean War.

The missionaries's relations with Tewodros, however, soon afterwards turned sour, and Susan and Mary were among the European captives whom the Emperor imprisoned at his mountain fortress of Maqdala (Magdala) - an act which resulted in long diplomatic negotiations, and eventually in the British Maqdala Expedition of 1867-8. This led in its turn to the crushing defeat of the Ethiopian forces, followed by Tewodros's dramatic suicide, and the looting by the British troops of hundreds of Ethiopian manuscripts and other treasures….

~

Wega George's story then moves to Lebanon, where Theophilus Waldmeier, on leaving Ethiopia, becomes a Quaker, purchases land at Brummana, a tiny settlement above Beirut, builds a mission house and school - and persuades Karl and Mary Saalmüller to join him.

Time passes, and a new generation, scarcely less interesting than its predecessor, is born. Stephana Saalmüller, Mary Bell's daughter by Karl Saalmüller – perpetuating her mother's family's relationship with Ethiopia - marries a young British consular official, and travels with him to the country of her birth. He was none other than Charles Armbruster, who goes on to write a huge, still highly regarded, multi-volume dictionary of Amharic.

Stephana's sister Wega Saalmüller (the grandmother after whom our author is named) stays on in Lebanon . Though no more than a child she falls in love – as her letters bashfully testify – and marries the Quaker educationist Thomas Little. Despite a great disparity of age - he is two decades her elder - she dutifully helps him run his boys' training school.

Their daughter, Vera Little, continues the family's interest in the East – and its commitment to education, by teaching in Cairo, Egypt. There she marries the American educationist Theodore (or Ted) Miller, who studied theology at Princeton Theological Seminary - and later lectures at the American University in Cairo. He subsequently joins the American Navy, takes part, at the close of World War II, in the Normandy Landings – and is a supporter of the American Civil Rights movement.

~

Wega George's story, which comes vividly alive, thus covers four generations of dedication and many fields of service.

In Their Generations

In Their Generations

PROLOGUE

When I was very young and knew very little of myself at all, I knew that I had been adopted. From my new father I absorbed an ordered mind and a boundless love of books, but from his wife, my mother, I gained a family. It was a vastly romantic family that had descended from the royal house of Abyssinia and brushed against the Ustinovs of Russia. There were missionaries to foreign lands, a British Consul to Khartoum, and its founder was an English adventurer and explorer in Africa.

Mother would remember the various relatives to my brother and me on Sunday afternoons when we sat at the foot of her bed where she loved to relax, nibble petite beurres, and sip Lapsang Sou-chong tea. Her recollections were usually accurate, but sometimes they became richly embroidered with the colors and designs of family affection. Always there was wonder and pride in her recitations, and always we were the natural filial recipients of the family story.

Wega Miller George

Part I

John Bell

O, young Lochinvar is come out of the west,
Through all the wide Border his steed was the best;
And save his good broadsword, he weapons had none,
He rode all unarmed and he rode all alone.
So faithful in love and so dauntless in war,
There never was knight like young Lochinvar.
    —Sir Walter Scott

In Their Generations

Mid 19th Century Abyssinia

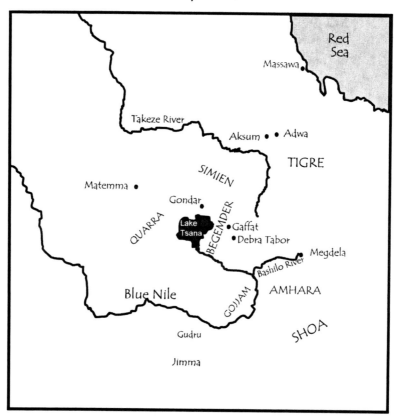

Wega Miller George

The story begins with John Bell. Of English parentage, he was born in Malta and, as a young man, served as a lieutenant in the British navy. I have water color miniatures of both his mother and his sister, each dressed in a dainty gown in the style known to the years of Napoleon's empire, and a portrait of his daughter in her wedding cloak richly embroidered in pure gold, but of himself there is nothing. I must imagine a young, English adventurer of the mid-nineteenth century. His sister had curly brown hair and pale blue eyes. Perhaps he mirrored these features. He was a romantic and a risk-taker; but not, according to his friend, King Theodore, well coordinated.

So many of John Bell's contemporaries kept diaries, particularly when they traveled. His frequent companion in Africa, Walter Plowden, wrote of his travels in Abyssinia and in the Galla country. Mansfield Parkyns wrote about his life in Abyssinia from notes he collected during a three years' stay. Earlier, Samuel Baker had written about his exploration of parts of the Blue Nile; and later, Hormutz Rassam kept a detailed daily account of his four-year sojourn to the court of King Theodore. Bell's son-in-law, Theophilus Waldmeier, kept records of his life in Abyssinia from 1858 to 1868. Bell himself was highly literate. He always carried with him a well-worn volume of his beloved Shakespeare and was skilled in Eastern languages. He, too, kept journals, in particular a journal of his travels in Abyssinia from the years 1840 through 1842; but to my knowledge only a few pages from these writings have been published and survive. Still, even these few, tantalizing pages clearly speak of a consummate nineteenth century explorer and adventurer. Walter Plowden described his own desire for travel as "...simply for the love of change, and of the wildest freedom...." (10, p. 234.) John Bell's life embodied this cultural obsession.

~

We first hear of John Bell as a participant in an amazing expedition to find a shortcut between the industrial activity of England and the raw materials found in India. Going from the Mediterranean to the Red Sea by way of a canal was certainly talked about; but a certain Captain in the British Army, one Francis Rawdon Chesney, envisioned a more direct route across Syria to Birecik in Turkey and then all the way down the Euphrates River by steamboat to Basra and out to the Persian Gulf.

Chesney's plan was to carry two large paddle steamboats overland, in pieces, to the Euphrates River and there to assemble them and cruise downstream, charting a course. The overland trek, accomplished with enormous difficulty, traversed mountains, swampland and the desert; but by February of 1836, the travelers reached the river. When the two ships were assembled they carried a notably eclectic group. The historical writer, John Brinton, tells us that on the larger ship, named the *Euphrates*, were a German Botanist and his wife, twenty-two officers and scientists, thirteen Arab seamen, an American cook and an Iraqi translator. The smaller ship, the *Tigris*, carried twenty officers and scientists, twelve Arab seamen and "...Mr. John Bell who was later known as 'Theodore's Englishman'..." (5, p. 3)

For two months the ships crept down the Euphrates, confronting the hazards of unmapped waters and the accidental loss of the barge carrying their supply of coal. Still, they were able to navigate the river, and the sights along the way included ancient castles and a fascinating range of wildlife.

Then suddenly, on the 21st of May, the sky took on a peculiar color and quickly darkened, with acres of sand blowing in the air. Chesney ordered both vessels to shore, but by this time the wind was blowing at hurricane force. The *Euphrates* managed to land and tie up, but when the *Tigris* hit the bank of the river she did so with such force that she ricocheted back out into the current. Within minutes she capsized and sank, taking twenty-one men with her. Somehow a very few survived the ordeal and among them was my great, great grandfather, John Bell. Within minutes the storm passed over and the sun came out, but that was the end of the British shortcut route to India. (5, p. 5)

Bell went back to Syria where he served briefly as the British Consul at Aleppo. It was here that he conceived of the notion of traveling to Africa. My Mother's aunt, Stephana Armbruster, (known to the family as Auntie Fana) tells us that John Bell, like so many of his co-patriots, was energized by the vision of seeing for himself the source of the Nile. She puts the date at about 1850; but by that time, according to his own journal, Bell had already been in Abyssinia for ten years.

~

If the designation of Abyssinia, as opposed to Ethiopia, seems quaint; I use it advisedly. My understanding is that Abyssinia was a smaller geographic area than Ethiopia. Although all of the borders have changed in the interim, in the middle of the nineteenth century, Abyssinia was understood to comprise chiefly the three principalities of Tigre, Amhara and Shoa; and it is the term that so many of the early travelers used.

Indeed, Abyssinia was unique in Africa. It was an isolated

bastion of Christianity in a continent of Islam and of primitive animism. Even its Christianity was distinctive, being a branch of the Orthodox Church which had retained a large jolt of Judaism from the indigenous population. Geographically, the country was practically unassailable. It enjoyed highlands of unimaginable beauty, comfort and fertility; and mountain peaks ranging to 15,000 feet. In his description of the British campaign to rescue the European captives in 1868, Henry Stanley describes the landscape with wonder:

"The higher we ascend the grander the scene! Under a sky of gorgeous sunshine, as blue as ever vaunted Italy boasted, spreads the wildest land, growing each day wilder and more rugged as we advanced.... The mountain tops are tinged with the brightest colours of the solar light." (11, p. 384)

The dawn of the nineteenth century revealed Abyssinia in feudal disarray. Centuries of rule by an imperial family had ended some decades previously. The fabled royalty, reputed to have descended from the union of the Queen of Sheba and Israel's Solomon, had fallen; and its remnants eked out their political lives at the pleasure of local chiefs. (8, p.1) There was no central power and the divided government suffered from endless disputes and inefficiencies. Both travelers of that time and historians have compared the society to feudal days in Briton "…when the great barons were followed to war by all born on their lands, and by their followers. Allowing for the poverty of the country, and the less stern and ferocious character of its inhabitants, you have, in Abyssinia, the picture of those times." (10, p. 51) Traveling through the country in 1863, the Englishman, Henry Dufton, observed, "It will be a matter of great difficulty to unite all the disconnected particles, of which the political state of this country consists, into one kingdom or empire, accustomed as the people have been for ages to recognize in a king nothing but the name of majesty." (7, p. 208) When John Bell arrived in 1840 the three major provinces –

Tigre, Amhara and Shoa – were governed by Dejazmach (Lord) Wube; Queen Menen and her son, Ras Ali; and King Sellase respectively. These major provinces, with their feudal lords, were virtually independent.

There is no record of Bell's immediate impressions of the country, but he does describe some of his early days in his journal. We first find him in Gondar, just north of Lake Tsana, setting out in a southerly direction presumably in conjunction with his purpose to see for himself the source of the Nile. It is March of 1841. Upon sighting the northern shore of the Lake he sees, with delight, his first hippopotamus basking in the sun on a shoal. Further along, at the top of a range of hills to the east of his road, Bell espies the ruins of Emfras and ponders upon this sad emblem of a royal family whose power has dwindled away. He travels comfortably by mule attended by a few servants and in the company of a group of Arab merchants. Usually prudent, Bell tries to travel through the countryside within groups as, with the lack of a central government, bandits are legion. The men continue southward, with Lake Tsana on the right and the hills leading to Debra Tabor on the left. On short stops to rest the mules, the Arabs brew coffee and Bell takes a gun and shoots guinea fowl and a small deer for food. The deer is eaten raw by Bell's Abyssinian servants, who protest it is far better so, than cooked.

The next day the little group arrives at the market town of Efag where, before noon, thousands of people mill about enjoying the wares and the bustling activity. Efag is particularly noted for livestock, and Bell purchases two handsome mules for 390 pieces of salt each, bars of salt being the denomination of currency as a subset of the silver Maria Teresa coin. In Efag he meets an earlier acquaintance who is en route to Korata and the man agrees to allow Bell and his men to join his traveling group, but at the appointed time and place of meeting Bell discovers that these men have already departed. With only four

Abyssinians in train, including his faithful attendant Gabriote, Bell hastens to follow, knowing the danger of a lonely and unfamiliar road.

He soon gives up hope of overtaking the larger company and determines to continue his course southward, always keeping parallel to Lake Tsana on his right. After two days the five men find themselves on a very lonely and wooded road. Bell is in the lead, on foot, with Gabriote and another one of his men about two hundred yards behind and the other two men bringing up the rear with the mules. He enters a narrow lane with high bushes on either side, and begins to walk very quickly. Just as he is about to emerge from this enclosed path, eight men armed with spears burst out of the shrubbery and knock him down. Bell's man, Gabriote, rushes to his side with sword in hand. By now Bell has leapt to his feet and fires his pistol, which misfires twice. Grabbing it by the muzzle he proceeds to use it as a club. In the meantime the three other members of Bell's party have vanished.

When the bandits see Gabriote rush to Bell's aid, they renew their advance, surrounding the two men and attacking with lances. Both Bell and Gabriote are severely wounded. One of the bandits brings his lance down with great force between Bell's eyes, blinding him with spurts of his own blood. In the footnotes to Bell's journal he describes the wound thus: "The lance was found to have entered the superior part of the nasal bones, to have pierced the superior palate bones and to have run along the superior maxillary bone finally making its exit just below the right ear..."! (3, p. 12) Meanwhile Gabriote, who has been bravely supporting Bell, begins to stagger from loss of blood. As he and Bell collapse, the bandits hastily leave, carrying the sword and the clothes that Bell and Gabriote had thrown aside for greater freedom of motion.

As soon as Bell orients himself he sees the ground about him covered with blood and that both he and Gabriote are in dire condition. With great difficulty they pull themselves upright and begin to walk toward Korata. Each one falls three or four times, but by now their other companions reappear to assist their progress. Korata turns out to be only half an hour away and, upon reaching the door of the church, they sink to the ground, insensible.

Fortunately a merchant friend, Ayto Cassai, appears and takes the two men to his home. But for his kindness, they would most likely have died. One of the first ministrations offered to Bell by the women of the house is a horn of tella, a sort of beer. Bell says that when he tried to drink it, to his great astonishment instead of going down his throat the tella poured out of the wound between his eyes, causing excruciating pain.

As Bell recovers both he and Ayto Cassai complain of the attack to the local ruler, Ras Ali; who hastens to see that the goods stolen from Bell are returned. But according to the peculiarities of the Abyssinian justice system, the Ras refuses to prosecute the bandits. His reasoning is that they too have suffered serious physical injuries, "…one having had his shoulder laid open by the sword, and the other his head with the butt of my pistol…." (3, p. 13) Bell leaves the Ras' court in disgust and returns to Ayto Cassai's home in Korata to continue his recuperation with poor Gabriote, who is still in a very precarious state.

~

On the second of April the town is agog with the arrival of Dejazmach Goshu. Bell admires this tribal chieftain as princely, both in appearance and in conduct – far more so than any other Abyssinian ruler he has met. Goshu has been required by Ras Ali to prove his loyalty by bringing fourteen thousand of his men to assist the Ras' mother, Queen Menen, against the rebellious tribe of the Agows. Bell and Ayto Cassai approach

Dejazmach Goshu to pay their respects and are invited to spend the day with him. In the course of the visit Goshu offers to take Bell along to see any part of his country that he might like to visit. Of course, Bell accepts.

On the fourth of April Bell sets out to join Dejazmach Goshu who is a short distance from Korata, his main body of troops being on the south side of the Nile about four hours away. Ayto Cassai has offered to accompany him for a day or so, and he gratefully agrees: his wound is still not well healed. They travel to the south, first fording a small stream and then entering hilly country from which they eventually descend to the Blue Nile (or the River Abbay). It has passed through the southeast corner of Lake Tsana some miles distant and has here become very wide and rapid, but still easy to ford when mounted on their mules. In another hour or so Dejazmach Goshu calls a halt for the night and orders huts built with branches of trees and rushes, a normal procedure. Only the Dejazmach himself has a tent. For the rest of the campaign Goshu's soldiers will construct a hut for Bell at each encampment. Ayto Cassai shares Bell's quarters for the night prior to returning to Korata the next day. It is very nearly Easter.

The expedition continues through the week, swinging along south of Lake Tsana and approaching the territory of the Agows. Four days before the Easter holiday they stop at the small and picturesque village of Ennagadi. Very early on the morning of Easter Sunday Dejazmach Goshu, with his chieftains, goes to the village church. It is odd that Bell does not go with them. Perhaps he was not asked. Years later Bell's children remembered with joy that on holy days the priests would come to their home and bless it, burn incense and sprinkle holy water, while their neighbors carried beautiful crosses and expressed their good wishes.

Upon Goshu's return from church he sends for Bell to participate in a brendo, or a feast, which he is to give for his chiefs and soldiers. Bell is first to arrive, and is seated on an animal skin which has been spread especially for him. Soon after taking his place Goshu's chieftains enter and each takes his place according to his rank. There are two long tables set up with various breads and choice dishes. Abyssinian cooking usually contained large quantities of peppers and other spices. Bell then tells us that, "...three or four oxen were thrown down before the door, killed, skinned and cut up with incredible dispatch. The best pieces were chosen and handed about while still quivering." (3, p. 17) The first piece is naturally given to Goshu, who proceeds to section it with his knife and serve a choice morsel to John Bell. With infinite grace Bell rises and receives the meat with both hands, bowing low, as is the custom, and proceeds to eat, assuring us that dipped into the various sauces it is really quite good. It is a great honor to be served by the chieftain's hands – even greater if he puts the food directly into your mouth. Goshu continues to serve Bell throughout the meal, which concludes with grilled ribs.

The Chieftains then retire, making room for a second group of diners consisting of soldiers. They, in turn, are followed by the last group that is composed of all sorts of stragglers. These quickly finish off the remains of the feast and are turned out by the Chamberlain. The meal is followed by mead, and musicians come to sing the praises of the Chief and of all who have fought bravely. The celebration continues until dark, when Bell retires to his hut.

Suddenly there is a loud shouting and the sound of horses galloping and guns firing. Evidently the mead has had its effect and the soldiers and chiefs have gathered in front of Dejazmach Goshu's tent to recall battles they have fought and won in order to firm their resolve for their pending war against the Agows. The scene is wonderfully wild and exciting with the men in their savage war dress, carrying weapons and galloping back and forth with extraordinary panache. The next morning, Easter

Monday, they are all back in church.

Early on Tuesday they break camp and the men continue their march along Lake Tsana, now to the west and northwest. Later, they pitch camp on the banks of the River Tull and, as it is still early, Goshu proposes target practice with Bell. This time his pistol is working. By now Goshu has integrated Bell into his household where he participates in all meals and other activities. About midnight the rain is falling in torrents. His hut being no better than a sieve, Bell sits outside on a stump huddled under an animal skin. At dawn the group is once more on the move.

In the middle of the day they sight the rest of their army on the slope of a hill. When these men see Goshu and his staff coming, the various chiefs, with their men, dash down the hill to meet him. As Goshu approaches them they "...draw themselves up in a line, along the side of the road, bowing to their horses manes as the Dedjadj Mateh passe[s]. Then they set off galloping in every direction, throwing sticks at each other and shouting their war cries." (3, p. 20)

In the morning Bell asks Dejazmach Goshu if he may separate himself briefly from the army to visit the source of the Blue Nile, as it is reported to be only a day's march away. Goshu, knowing the area to be dangerous, denies permission as he cannot spare an escort; but promises that on their return Bell shall make the trip. Seemingly in compensation, he presents Bell with a beautiful shield decorated with gold and silver, and with the mane and tail of a lion. At dawn the next day the army continues westward and by noon they can see the deserted campfires of the Agows. Goshu's forces burn everything in sight, a typical tactic. Soon a herd of cattle is seen and a fierce fight with remnants of the Agow forces secures the animals to Goshu's men. The army dines heavily on beef that night.

On the next day Bell is witness to the simplicity and swiftness of Abyssinian justice. In a quarrel between some soldiers one of them, who is related to some of the more important men in the camp, happens to be killed by a spear wound to the stomach. The man guilty of the attack is immediately handed over to the victim's relatives who, with spears, dispatch him on the spot.

At ten o'clock the next morning Goshu's force comes in sight of Queen Menen's army and he is ceremoniously received and congratulated on his successes on the march. With the countryside now subdued Bell again requests permission to proceed to the area from which the Blue Nile first flows. This time Goshu readily accedes and sends for an official, Azi Weld Inchael, whose ancestral land is in the area of the source of the Nile. He is charged with Bell's safety and told to escort him wherever he may chose to go. Goshu arranges their departure for the next day and, with the gift of a handsome mule, assures Bell of a warm welcome whenever he may choose to return.

Now Bell is at last close to the consummation of his purpose in coming to Abyssinia. His strong desire to see the remote beginnings of the Blue Nile has driven him this far and his excitement builds. At the bottom of a hill he and Azi Weld Inchael meet about six hundred men who are headed for Damot, and they join them in their trip southward. In Abyssinia one always best travels in company. They pass ambas (flat mountain tops) from which remnants of the Agow army look down upon them, but do not hinder their passage. The countryside is dreadfully damaged and villages burned. In the evening they find a small Agow village that has escaped destruction. Now, far from the lines of battle, they are received kindly and dine on lamb and beer. At dawn they continue their southerly journey, having distanced themselves from all signs of warfare. The land is hilly, wooded and intersected by numerous streams; and crops are plentiful. At noon Azi Weld Inchael sends the baggage and most of their men on to his home in Saccala, retaining only thirty guards as an escort. They turn slightly westward and descend into a broad valley. At the bottom of the valley is an open space of marshy ground and near a cluster of trees there is a pool of water two feet in diameter.

Here, as Bell tells us, was "the sole object of my ambition". (3, p. 22) The ground around the pool was very soft and wet. One of the escort, to demonstrate the depth of the moisture, shoves his lance into the marshy ground and it simply disappears. In an instant he sheds his clothes and dives head first into the muck, with his peers grabbing on to his feet as he submerges. Upon finding his weapon, his compatriots pull him out – quite unabashed by his sudden bath.

As the day draws to a close each soldier sprinkles a little of the water on his head, believing in its fortuitous powers, and Azi Weld Inchael presents Bell with a horn of the liquid to drink. In the shadows they climb a hill toward the church of Gish Kudder Michael. Bell turns to impress the view on his memory, deeply moved at having attained his goal. Each man kisses the post of the door of the little church, and the group proceeds through a wooded country and crosses the infant Nile just below the point at which it turns northward to flow toward Lake Tsana. Passing over mountainous country for a short while, they reach Azi Weld Inchael's home where they gratefully stop to rest for the night. Within a few days Bell returns to the home of his kind friend, Ayto Cassai, at Korata. Three years later another friend, Walter Plowden, describes this same approach to Korata with the moon bursting forth

"…in one instant in full splendour over the lake (Tsana),… defining beautifully a small island in the bay, with its church and trees, whose drooping foliage kissed their shadows; the hippopotami, pasturing in hundreds along the banks, were snorting and crushing among the reeds over one another; the wild boar, or startled deer, would dash at speed across the path; and the roar of the lion, growing more noble and impressive as the distance increased, came swooping down from time to time, answered by the harsher and more startling roar of another.…"

(10, p. 191)

Is it any wonder that somewhere between the time that he arrived in Abyssinia in 1840, and his trek to the source of the Blue Nile the next year, Bell has quite lost his heart to this unique and beautiful land?

~

There is one more event that Bell describes for us in the published pages of his journal. On February 25, 1842, a newly-appointed Abun arrives in Gondar, greeted with all of the pomp and ceremony that the church in Abyssinia can muster. The Abun (or head of the Abyssinian Church) is appointed for life by the Patriarch of the Coptic Church in Alexandria, Egypt. The residents of Gondar are dressed in their richest apparel - the men, in their war dress, mounted on horseback and the women, in their finest costumes, mounted on mules. As the Abun approaches a salute is fired and those on horseback draw up in a line along the roadside and bow to the manes of their animals. There are musicians riding mules on which kettle drums are fastened and others, playing on reeds, marching in groups of three. Bell and a few other Europeans who are present walk along side of the Ichege Guebra Mariam, a native of Abyssinia and head of its religious orders. Next to the Abun, he is the greatest religious dignitary in the country. The Ichege rides on a beautiful white mule. He wears a purple robe and his saddle and harness are of purple velvet decorated with gold and silver. On his head is a white turban covered with a piece of white muslin which falls gracefully over the hind quarters of his mule. A large purple umbrella with a massive silver fringe shades the Abun. Carrying a silver cross he blesses the crowd as he passes. Both the Abun and the Ichege are fully covered with cashmere shawls that are removed at the same moment when they meet. There are shouts of joy from the crowd and gay ululations from the women. (3, pp. 23-25)

~

We next hear of John Bell in July of 1843. As far as I can discover this is the only instance when he left the boundaries of Abyssinia from the time he arrived in 1840 until his untimely death in 1860. For reasons that I do not know, he was on board a steam packet in the Red Sea headed for Suez, Egypt. In the course of this voyage he met an Englishman, James Crawford, who seems to have been so intrigued by Bell's travels that he subsequently wrote about them to the Royal Geographical Society in London. Crawford describes John Bell to us as "tall, strong and intelligent, but seemingly uninterested … to bring himself forward by writing or giving any account of his travels…" and suggests that the Society might be interested in sending someone to interview Bell in order to record his experiences. He continues, saying that "… (Bell) had had several encounters with robbers & others & was wounded in several places & altogether his story was most romantic." (6)

While in Suez, Bell encounters Walter Plowden who is en route from India, where he has been employed by a trading firm, back home to England. Evidently, his sedentary duties in the mercantile world have left him restless and, upon meeting Bell, he straightaway casts aside any other plans that he might have had and, without any preparation, returns with him to Abyssinia. The two young men become great friends, but it is interesting to compare their very different approaches to life in the country. Plowden, more ambitious, eventually negotiates his skills to become the British Consul in Abyssinia. Bell, integrating himself into the land and its people, becomes the King's first minister.

Wega Miller George

~

John Bell and Walter Plowden sailed back down the Red Sea and reentered Abyssinia through the Port of Massawa where, unfortunately, they both came down with malaria. The normal route inland took them through Adwa and Aksum (the ancient capital in Tigre) and on across high ranges of mountains to Amhara, but Plowden is able to travel only three days before he becomes too ill to continue. Bell makes him as comfortable as possible at Kiaquor, a village just over the first range of mountains, and continues on to Adwa to prepare a place for him at their next stop. At this point a third Englishman, Mansfield Parkyns, comes into the picture for a little while, and we have rather a delightful image of three young men, probably all in their mid to late twenties, on a high adventure. Accidentally hearing of Parkyns' arrival in the country, Plowden sends a message begging him to join him. Parkyns hastens to Kiaquor where he finds his friend much improved and able to continue on to Adwa to meet Bell. From there the three, with their small retinue and in spite of bouts of fever, continue inland; now with the additional discomfort of the advancing rainy season. Each evening they seek shelter in whatever hamlet or village may be nearby. Parkyns describes one such night in Addy Argoud:

"We passed a very uncomfortable night. The pouring rain obliged us to sleep in the hut, which we seldom did when weather permitted us to remain outside. We managed to procure a stretcher for Plowden; but Bell and I lay together on the medabe or mud couch, which is in every house. Scarcely, however, had we begun to think of rest, when myriads of bugs which crawled over us made us get up again. Having lighted a lamp ... we proceeded to examine the state of the wall and our couch, and found both literally blackened with these disgusting insects, which ran about till the whole place appeared alive .... Seeing that all hope of rest inside was in vain, we rolled

ourselves up in skins, and slept outside in the mud and rain." (9, pp. 69-70)

Upon reaching Adwa Parkyns strikes out on his own to the remote regions of the northern frontier of Tigre. Bell and Plowden continue on their way to Gondar, and from there to the court of Ras Ali at Debra Tabor. They arrive early in 1844, and remain in this general area making it the center for various peregrinations.

~

In the month of June, 1845, Bell is in Yawish, in an area of Basso, just north of Gojjam, arranging a trip south to the Galla Country, which is separated from Abyssinia by the Blue Nile. The trip is simply to be an adventure and visit to the reputedly warlike tribes south of the Nile. Their projected destination is the Galla district of Gudru, and a local Basso chief, who has influential relatives in Gudru has promised to assist them. A large group of merchants has already departed, agreeing to welcome Bell and Plowden whenever they can meet up with them in southern Gudru. There are only three days remaining before the rainy season will render the Nile impassable, and the two young men hasten their departure. The friendly Basso chief will provide a Galla named Govala to serve as their guide to the caravan. He urges them to carry an ample supply of guns. Both Bell and Plowden demur, knowing that visible firearms can quickly lead to challenges and disputes, but they do each stash a single matchlock to provide defense against wild animals and game for the cooking pot.

Leaving early in the morning they soon come to the lovely, fertile plain of Gojjam which borders on the Blue Nile. The view is expansive, looking down, ever downward, until the hills covered with trees seem to be a misty plain, and a line of clouds covers the gorge in which courses the Nile. Then beyond this invisible ravine "... a similar expanse of undulating ridges rose at once, at some eight miles distance, into the bold ranges of the Gallas, purple, and well-defined in the clear atmosphere, their broad tops marked freely against the sky, at nearly the same level as that on which we were standing." (10, p. 281) As their little group descends toward the river, alternately riding their mules or scrambling down the more precipitous ridges on foot, it gradually accumulates groups of spearmen, merchants, Gallas and market people until it has swollen in number to nearly a thousand. Upon reaching the river they find it swarming with Gallas floating their market goods across from the other side, shouting and yelling, the sounds echoing from the sides of the gorge. All is noise and bustle, and the river rolls strongly along. The sand under their bare feet is roasting, but the excitement of the scene erases all discomfort.

When their guide, Govala, and his brother have maneuvered all of the party's goods across, Bell and Plowden hasten to go over before sunset, when the crocodiles will become more bold. Upon completing their crossing they light a small fire on the sand and spread animal skins on which to sleep. There has been some talk of guns and the two young men are somewhat apprehensive, but as Plowden notes, "...return was now impracticable, and fear useless." (10, p. 284) Their rest is uneasy.

At first light and with their small party, Bell and Plowden begin the steep ascent up out of the Nile gorge. As they go up the land slowly levels off. There is a brief alarm that there are Kootlai Gallas in the vicinity about to attack, and each in the little party snatches up his shield; but the rumor is false. Soon a group of Gallas does appear and there are heated discussions between them and the guide, Govala. Again, the two young men hear the Galla word for guns. The dispute ends peaceably and their course leads them to a pleasant, level country, green and fertile, with picturesque beehive shaped huts and carefully delineated fields. The air is bucolic as they reach the home of Govala where they will rest for the night. They sup on injera (flat bread made with the grain called teff) and curds mixed with cayenne-like peppers, and are given beer to drink.

The next morning Bell and Plowden are anxious to proceed toward their rendezvous with the merchant caravan in southern Gudru, but Govala tells them it is impossible to travel across the adjacent land belonging to Alemanu Dillu without his permission. After four days of waiting they strike out anyway, but are driven back by an unknown Galla with the butt end of his lance. Their host, Govala, appears bemused; but it is apparent that some chicanery is afoot. Bell and Plowden are allowed to continue on their way, but with all the talk of guns, they decide to leave their two weapons hidden in the home of an ancient Abyssinian whom they have met along the way. Also, finding themselves encumbered by the number of their servants, they send four back to Govala. The following afternoon the illusive Alemanu intercepts them. This tall, powerful Galla is nevertheless cheerful and reassuring, and takes them to his home for the night. With Alemanu as their guide the next day, they proceed on toward southern Gudru. The sun shines on green fields and the lovely countryside is dotted with livestock. The air is clear, and magnificent birds decorate the noble landscape. All uneasiness evaporates in the thralls of nature's loveliness. Arriving at Alemanu's principal home, they are made comfortable and are in the happy glow of youth and adventure.

Bell and Plowden remain with Alemanu for a day or two waiting for their next guides to lead them on. These two, Gulama and Kustee, are sons of an illustrious chief in Gudru, but apparently they have been tied up in local warfare with the Jimma, a name that our two heroes are only just beginning to hear. When the two brothers eventually do appear, the reason for all of the glitches in the Englishmen's journey and the talk of guns is instantly apparent. From their early conversations with the Basso chief in Yawish and his assignment of their guide, Govala, Bell and Plowden have unwittingly been enticed to the Galla country to provide guns and leadership in the Gudru's ongoing battles with the Jimma. The two Gudrus tell Bell and Plowden that their homes have been burnt and all has been sorrow and despair, but now that the Englishmen have come to lead them, all is joy. Bell and Plowden quietly and firmly decline. They have no guns: they are travelers, not soldiers.

Leaving the Gudru's hut they sit outside under a large berbeesa tree and talk with Alemanu, who paints a clear picture of their predicament. He explains that all who have helped them on their way have anticipated that Bell and Plowden, with guns blazing, will lead them against the Jimma. When Gulama and Kustee come outside; they warn that they know that Bell and Plowden have guns and assert that these weapons must be used to enable them to conquer the Jimma. If the two Englishmen assist them, the Gudru will fall at their feet; if not, the alternative for Bell and Plowden will be dire. The Gudru are desperate men. By dark, Bell and Plowden find themselves imprisoned in a roofless hut with no fire or candle and only a little bread. It is raining. Their mules are kept away from any grass and their few servants are fearful of starvation.

There is now no hope of intercepting the merchant caravan. Their animals are hungry and they themselves are kept on short rations. Daily, the Gudru Gallas harass them about their guns – sometimes cajoling and sometimes threatening. At last, seeing no other course open to them, the two friends capitulate. Bell agrees to stay with Gulama and Kuskee as a hostage while Plowden retraces their steps to the home of the ancient Abyssinian to recover their two guns, "... one single-barrelled and the other double-barrelled, with a hammer of Abyssinian workmanship that frequently missed fire,... and what little powder, lead, and caps I had." (10, p. 293) Gratifying Alemanu by shooting a guinea fowl, Plowden returns to the Gudru enclave where Bell has been well cared for and where they are now entertained with generous enthusiasm. It is some comfort that they will direct the fight they cannot avoid. Having succumbed to the inevitable, Bell and Plowden send a message to the Jimma suggesting that they find some other locale for their combative activity, and settle in with the Gudru for the remainder of the rainy season.

Nearly two months go by quietly when suddenly, one afternoon; there is a Jimma attack on a village about a quarter of a mile away. The noise of men running, horses galloping and women shrieking is so intense that it appears that the Jimma are upon them. With their natural instincts in play, Bell and Plowden with their few Abyssinian servants grab their spears and rush toward the noise. To protect themselves the two Englishmen snatch up their guns and soon find themselves close to nearly five hundred Jimma horsemen. In the confusion the friends are separated. Plowden hears three shots across the field and realizes that Bell has not hit anything. Turning, he sees one of his Abyssinians covering him with his shield and a group of Jimma surrounding them. At a little distance are two Gudru chiefs looking aghast, while the rest have left the field. Sighting one opportunity, Plowden fires at the leading horseman and the first barrel of his gun misfires. Before the Jimma can rush, Plowden fires the second barrel and the Jimma warrior falls dead. At that instant the Gudru horsemen rush forward to sweep the disordered Jimma from the field. The Jimma have lost a renowned chief. When Bell and Plowden meet again on the field the Jimma are in full retreat. The reality is that at some unexpected time, in the not very distant future, they will return to seek revenge with their cavalry well multiplied.

The better part of valor now is to show great delight and friendship toward the Gudru. If they in any way suspect that the Englishmen feel the least resentment for their enforced detention the Gudru could prevent the two friends from ever returning to

Abyssinia, and even turn them over to the Jimma. So Bell and Plowden become friendly with the Gudru chiefs and even integrate themselves so well into the local society as to adopt their customs. They accept two horses, agreeing with the Gudru that the Jimma are too dangerous to face on foot; but only decline to become chiefs themselves. Another month passes.

Then comes the inevitable day. Bell and Plowden are in the company of about one hundred Gudru horsemen who are escorting tribal herdsmen to lead cattle to pasture when suddenly, over a slight rise in the land, appear more than three thousand Jimma horsemen racing at full speed across the plain. These warriors create a savage spectacle, with long hair streaming, animal skins flapping on their shoulders and lance points glistening in the sun. Seeming to have erupted from the earth, their wild screams rend the air.

The mounted chiefs do not hesitate and immediately push forward to meet the charge, while the men on foot urge the cattle to the rear. More Gudru horsemen arrive and the enemy is met. Once again it is their Abyssinian servants who draw Bell and Plowden into the battle. Very soon, the Jimma seem to recognize the two Englishmen, and rapidly begin a pincer movement in their direction. The Gudru facing the Jimma are forced to turn to escape being surrounded, and roar back to the spot where Bell and Plowden are standing. The Jimma cavalry are in heavy pursuit, their horses pounding the earth and their war cries filling the air. For an instant the two friends who have taken up position behind the retreating Gudrus turn to face the Jimma, when suddenly they see the two arms of the pincer motion closing in. They race to follow the Gudru and barely escape being captured. Then the three portions of the Jimma army close in to one body, roaring down a precipitous slope at full speed. Glancing behind them Bell and Plowden see one of their Abyssinians about to be struck and a group of Jimma not fifteen yards behind them. Their man is hit with a lance cut across the shoulder, while at the same time their Gudru companions urge their flight.

They are appalled to be leaving their own man to certain death. They have hatched this mad adventure and their men have followed them faithfully. Both Bell and Plowden wheel their horses about, and the five Gudru chiefs with them follow. Surprise seems to catch the Jimma off balance and before they can right themselves Plowden fires the double barreled gun. One bullet hits a Jimma chief in the wrist so that he drops his lance, and the other hits a second chief in the side. Simultaneously, Kustee (one of the Gudru brothers who has tricked the Englishmen into battle) hurls his spear at a third warrior and pins his shield with his arm to his side. Shouting and pushing forward Bell, Plowden and the five chiefs force the foremost Jimma to turn. Having given the remaining Gudrus cover to cross a creek to safety, the seven men then turn and quickly follow.

The Jimma ride up, throw their lances in challenge and race off. The Gudru, who are now on their home ground, rush to give battle. Bell and Plowden are switching guns to reload and notice with horror that vultures and kites are now flying through the melee to light on still palpitating bodies. Plowden fires Bell's gun and hits one of the Jimma racing off on his horse. By great good fortune this man is the preeminent Jimma chief, and his death stills the Jimma's lust for war. (10, pp. 290-304)

By now Bell and Plowden have entirely convinced the Gudru chiefs that they have acted with them out of their great love and respect for them. Only by having acquired a strong influence over the chiefs are they allowed to leave at the end of February, 1846. Their departure is accompanied by tears of gratitude and affection. The two young men attain the ford at the Nile on the very earliest day possible after the rains for a safe crossing, and appear on the northern side to the great amazement of the chief of Basso and of their own friends, who had long given them up for dead. They are soon safely back in Amhara at the court of Ras Ali. By October Plowden is on his way to

England. Bell has settled in for the long haul.

~

It was at about this time that John Bell married. He had adopted the country: now he would wed one of its daughters. Auntie Fana tells us that Bell married Woisero (the Lady) Worqenesh Asfaw Yilma. My mother always assumed that she was a member of King Theodore's family and Fana writes that she was a cousin of the King. Indeed, the relationship that I have been able to discover is that Worqenesh was the daughter of Asfaw Yilma, the Dejazmach of the Province of Begemder. He had married a niece of King Theodore. It is easier simply to think of Worqenesh as a daughter of a noble family who lived in the mountains above Debra Tabor. It seems to have been a love match. Over the years three children were born. There was a son, named for his father, of whom I never heard in my childhood and who remains an enigma to me to this day. And there were two girls – Susan Jewubdar (the limit of beauty) and my great grandmother, Mary Belletech (beyond the limit of beauty). They lived in the village of Diddim, which was in the area of his wife's family home and was given to Bell by Ras Ali. Their house, not far from Debra Tabor, stood on a very high hill – part of a mountain range where the cold and fogs were reminiscent of Scotland. The sides of the mountains were covered in fir trees, and it scarcely seemed credible that they were in Africa at all.

In Plowden's absence Bell becomes a part of the royal court of Ras Ali. We have already seen Bell as a traveler with Dejazmach Goshu's campaign to reinforce Queen Menen's fight against the Agow. Now he attends her son, and is given the rank of Basha (captain). The state of the Christian highlands in Abyssinia is one of continuous tribal warfare. In 1847, when Plowden is on his way to England, Queen Menen and Ras Ali are recognizing the growing power of a young, free-lance soldier from Quarra, Dejazmach Kassa Haylu. An expedition to crush him has failed. Instead, Ras Ali has been forced to appoint him as a provincial governor and arrange a marriage between Kassa and his daughter, Tewabach. Ali is still preeminent, and seeks trade with the outside world to accumulate weapons and military skills. Plowden has taken his intimate knowledge of Abyssinia back to England, and returns to Debra Tabor in 1849 bearing a political agreement. He has persuaded the English government to appoint him as Consul to Abyssinia (in the person of Ras Ali) and he goes straight to the Ras's residence at Debra Tabor, where Bell hurries from Diddim to meet him.

Herein begins an astonishing cat and mouse chase to secure the Ras' signature on the treaty with England. To attain entry to the Ras' presence they have to traverse layers of protocol. Ras Ali's house is the only stone edifice in the city. Day and night numerous supplicants sit about it in appalling filth awaiting entrance, regardless of their social status. (Abyssinians could be refreshingly egalitarian.) Passing through this first barrier, Bell and Plowden enter a court where household servants sit, waiting for instructions from the Ras. Within minutes they are fortunate to break through ceremonial forms and are whisked into the Ras' presence and his entourage of workman and horses. Seated on animal skins on the floor, the two are constantly at risk of being stepped on. The Ras is pleased to see the two young men and immediately questions Plowden as to what gifts he has brought. Conversing pleasantly, Plowden coyly puts him off.

At noon the next day he and Bell carry a number of gifts to the Ras along with a letter from Queen Victoria. He reads Her Majesty's letter to Ras Ali, who seems unable to understand its purpose; and then distributes the gifts she has sent. The Ras finds it impossible to hide his amazement and gratification at the lavish display. Not wishing to press the Ras on the matter of the Treaty, Plowden retires with Bell to Diddim. Then begins an earnest discourse between the two camps, with the Ras sending to Plowden for more guns, pistols or anything else he deems desirable while Plowden begins to press him on the subject of the Treaty. The Ras continually puts him off while squeezing his resources dry, and then abruptly leaves on a campaign to Gojjam.

Caught off guard, Bell and Plowden hastily put together a month's worth of supplies which must include food, tents, cooking utensils, hides for beds, servants to grind corn and prepare the meals, mules to carry it all and fighting men to protect everything. Their party numbers close to a hundred. Off they rush to prevent being cut off from the Ras' army by hostile rear guard activity. En route they are joined by several chiefs also hurrying to overtake the Ras by forced marches. By the second day they find themselves near the Blue Nile where it exits Lake Tsana. Bell kills a hippopotamus. Plowden tells us that, "[h]ere are vast forests bordering on the great river, where wild beasts roam at leisure in a perpetual shade, and here and there meadows, clear and sunny; and beyond these the Nile spreads out in a wide and shining river." (10, p. 410) The poor man once more falls prey to malaria.

This time Bell and Plowden will cross the Nile by way of an ancient stone bridge, built by the Portuguese in the sixteenth century. The Ras has preceded them by one day. Their expanded party pushes forward with all of the typical disorder and good humor of an Abyssinian march, and soon reaches the Ras' camp near Agata. There is no stopping here. The Ras moves on across the River Ava. The descent to the river is through a three hundred foot cut and down a steep and slippery path over dead animals that have fallen – then on across the river, now only two feet in depth, but flowing swiftly. They scramble up the incline on the other side to the welcome sight of a wide plain where there is grazing for their animals and the Ras' tent is in sight. Next Ras Ali pushes forward to the mountainous province of Nephsee where Birru Goshu's troops are reported to be massing.

The rainy season has set in, which increases everyone's discomfort. Food is scarce. Birru Goshu has ravished the countryside and there are no supplies to be had anywhere. Then, to everyone's great joy, the Ras leaves Nephsee for the more clement environment of central Gojjam. There are forced marches in order to cross the numerous rivers on the way, before the rains make them impassable. Everyone pushes through the rain, mud and the swollen rivers – wading and swimming – and the Englishmen's party safely reaches Daveet, the sight of Ras Ali's newest camp.

Plowden has recovered from his fever, but now the very serious problem is the food supply which is quite dependent on Ras Ali. There are no markets and nothing to be bought so that the whole camp is, in the usual Abyssinian modus operandi, billeted upon the countryside. Bell reminds the Ras that Plowden has been ill and is in serious need of nourishment, and Ras Ali gives the two Englishmen three villages to act as a food source. The villages are widely separated and, of course, deserted. One is in the Valley of Kumbat, perhaps the most wild and beautiful of the provinces bordering the Blue Nile. From the highlands of Gojjam,

"... *precipitous cliffs hedge [the Nile] ... in all round, with only a difficult track here and there; over these thunder the rivers in the floods, sending their spray higher than the cliffs above, and generally wrapt in fog. After descending the first declivity, there is a succession of plateaux, well cultivated and woody, with intervening cliffs, several feet in height; and then over rough and broken ground – sometimes precipitous, sometimes a slope, sometimes stretching into a wide plain for miles – you reach the last descent to the Nile, which rolls 800 or 1000 feet below, almost hidden from the eye, the precipices being clothed with thick jungle.*" (10, p. 414)

On one of the plateau is a village assigned to the Englishmen. The houses are quite empty, but Bell espies an old man and is able to converse with him. He, in turn, encourages his neighbors to return. Bell and Plowden are kept awake all night by the thunder of the river and the noise of falling rocks. There are leopards nearby roaring and grunting, and the rain falls continuously.

Bell, fed by the reassured villagers, remains in the area for three months, while Plowden retires to Yawish. Only twice do they venture to Ras Ali's camp. Going by horseback they travel the fifteen miles across six rivers to Daveet. They retire to their respective retreats, thoroughly soaked, having swum across some of the rivers and forded others, and still Plowden has not persuaded the Ras to sign the treaty with England. As the rains slack off in September, Bell and Plowden hear a report that the Ras is about to return to Debra Tabor. Traveling through the plains of Gojjam they cross a high range of mountains beautifully covered with vast pine forests and eventually stumble upon the Ras' camp, where they are graciously welcomed. They are nearly back at the first Nile crossing. At long last Ras Ali, exhibiting extreme boredom, consents to another reading of the Treaty. Amid yawns and maddening inattention he announces that he can see no harm in the document and signs, muttering that the whole agreement appears utterly useless. With the country's geography, when will a serious English merchant ever grace its boundaries? He sends a copy of the papers to Debra Tabor to be locked up with other state papers. The year is 1849. Undoubtedly the Treaty was burned in 1853 when Dejazmach Kassa plundered and burned Ras Ali's home. (10, pp. 401-424)

~

Now the stage is set for a new player upon the Abyssinian scene, and now the very heart of John Bell's service to Abyssinia begins. In the early 1850's Ras Ali is still the ostensible ruler of the country, with reluctant acknowledgement from Wube of Tigre to the north of Amhara and open rebellion from Birru Goshu in Gojjam to the south. To the east, Shoa is somewhat removed from the endless inter-tribal warfare of the Christian Highlands, and has been ruled by the same family for over four decades.

Into this mix bursts Dejazmach Kassa Haylu, a son of the governing family of Quarra, a small western province bordering on the Sudan. The location is important because early in his life it schools Kassa in defensive maneuvers against the encroaching Egyptians. His father's brother was the governor of Quarra; his mother's background more uncertain, and ever a sensitive subject to him. Some said that in hard times she had peddled kosso (the local herbal cure for tapeworm), others that she was directly descended form the Queen of Sheba. Kassa had been raised in a monastery (significant because of his later passion for theological expression) and exploded onto the military scene in the late 1840's, necessitating Ras Ali's conciliatory offer of his daughter in marriage.

Kassa is a study in paradox – tyrannical and generous, utterly cruel and compassionate (on campaigns he would stop at river crossings, dismount and personally assist women and children to cross in safety) a notable military genius and foolhardy in administrative matters. He had enormous ambition, expecting to extend his power beyond Abyssinia to the protection of Jerusalem. His early years on the political scene were intoxicating to his adherents; it seemed that his potential was boundless. As his military successes accumulated people were drawn to his cause, and his bravery and talent for warfare secured their loyalty. In the civil wars following Kassa's marriage to Tewabach, and frequently spurred on by her encouragement, he strengthened his position until in 1853 he defeated Ras Ali at a battle on the plain near Ayshal. On that day John Bell fought at the side of Ras Ali and, at the close of the battle, he took refuge in a local church. Upon hearing that there was a European taking sanctuary nearby Kassa sent for him, promising him succor. Indeed, this time, Kassa kept his word and a friendship ensued.

My Auntie Fana describes their relationship as an extraordinary attachment. In those early years Kassa was a man whom one could love. The two would sit for hours together, Bell describing European civilization – the cities of London and Paris, the law, the fleets and armies, art, manufacturing, the peace and freedom of social life and the privacy of homes. Often Bell would pull out his cherished volume of Shakespeare and read to Kassa. Fana describes the two as interacting as equals, Bell recognizing Kassa's power and chiding his frailties. Particularly she cites one occasion when Bell has been offended by an injustice meted out to a man by a local court. In ancient Abyssinian tradition Bell dons full armor, mounts his horse and rides into Kassa's presence to berate him in strident terms. That evening, as he and Bell are about to sit down to dinner Kassa quits the tent, only to reappear wearing a large stone dangling from his neck. The tradition is to call out, "Pardon me, pardon me", until the offended party replies, "May God pardon thee". In a storm of remorse Bell rushes to Kassa to remove the rock from his neck. (1, p.4)

By 1854, as well as his family province of Quarra, Kassa rules Gondar and Amhara. Only Tigre and Shoa are still out of his grasp. Wube, of Tigre, is described by Plowden at this time as "… grave in manner, and of a piercing eye, silent and reserved, and much feared by all who approach him." (10, p. 389) He is loyal to friends and ruthless to enemies, and in business he is clever and quick. Wube has ruled in Tigre for many years, and now determines to make himself Emperor, but Kassa defeats him in the battle at Deresge and assumes the title for himself. He sends for the newly appointed Abun, Salama, who has come from Egypt to anoint Wube, and who now agrees to crown Kassa instead. With impressive political acumen Kassa chooses the imperial name of Tewodros, or Theodore; there being a well known prophesy in Abyssinia that the next ruler of that name will rule over the whole country, remove Islam from its borders and even capture the holy city of Jerusalem. So in February of 1855, Kassa is crowned Theodore II, and quickly begins to live up to his chosen cognomen.

At the time of his assumption of the royal thrown, Theodore was still young (in his thirties), vigorous and filled with visions of change and modernization for his country. He is described as of average height, sinewy and athletic. His complexion is dark for an Abyssinian and his features European, with a nose noticeably Roman. For many years a small portrait of Theodore, dressed in his usual garb of white cotton trousers with a long white over shirt, and carrying a spear, hung in my parent's home. It was flanked by two portraits of Bell's younger daughter, Mary, dressed in the royal robe Theodore had given to her for her wedding dress. I was more aware of Theodore than I was of John Bell.

Henry Blanc, who accompanied Hormuzd Rassam on his feckless journey to Abyssinia to free Britain's second consul, divides Theodore's career into three parts. The first encompasses his early years until the death of his much-loved first wife, Tewabach; the second spans the time from the fall of Ras Ali to the death of John Bell in 1860 and the third goes from that event until his own death in 1868. (4, p. 5) In the middle years, from 1855 to 1860 Theodore achieves great success, is much admired and struggles to accomplish various reforms. To replace the half naked dress of his people he introduces flowing trousers and long shirts. He reforms the structure of the military by paying his soldiers rather than setting them loose to ravish the countryside. A salaried military not only protects the land but creates loyalty. He also tries to bring a semblance of order and discipline to his troops. In this regard he places a thousand soldiers under John Bell's authority to be instructed in a European style of warfare. The experiment is hopeless. Most notably, recognizing the need for innovation in military matters, he introduces a sort of modest industrial revolution. He is particularly interested in the manufacture of gunpowder, cannon and mortar. Also in conjunction with military needs, he inaugurates an ambitious program of road building. He himself could often be seen on a construction site, directing the explosion of rocks and lifting those that were not crushed. Finally, perhaps of interest only to my family, he hoped to shore up the state of matrimony in the country, and tried to insist that only marriages performed at a church altar were valid. John Bell's in-laws so disliked Theodore that they refused to allow their daughter to succumb to his theological whims. Henry Blanc tells us that Bell was forced to wed a Galla slave in church, with the Emperor Theodore acting as the father of the bride. It was a sham. This is the only time that we hear of this unfortunate woman.

John Bell has now been in Abyssinia for more than fifteen years. When the missionary, Dr. Henry Stern, first visited the country in the 1850's he spoke of "…Mr. Bell, who was a perfect Abyssinian in appearance and dress, but a perfect gentleman in thought and heart…." (12, p 56) He seems to have been much loved by a great many. He and Plowden continued their close friendship. King Theodore depended on his knowledge and loyalty, giving Bell the rank of liqemekwas in the army (one of four officers who wore the same costume as the King in time of war). The distinction might seem dubious to us, but was a rank eagerly sought by chivalrous Abyssinians. Bell was constantly in camp with Theodore, and frequently slept across the door of his friend's tent. He was the only man whom the Emperor ever allowed to sit and share his meal from the same dish. But after the rainy season John Bell would go home to his family in Diddim for a while. Here, Fana tells us,

Theodore and his consort, escorted by a part of the army, would come to rest. Then Bell would take his three children and they would visit the royal couple for some days in their camp. (1. p. 4) In effect, Bell served as the Emperor's chamberlain, or first minister. The only criticism of Bell from Theodore that we ever hear is that he is too clumsy to learn how to fight with a shield.

Even during the promising first years of Theodore's reign, there were signs of rebellion. The reforms were not always easy to enforce – soldiers used to living off the local population found it difficult to break old habits. The King often had to fight to have his orders obeyed. He was frequently distracted with matters of jurisprudence. He found it difficult to delegate the resolution of legal suits, thinking of himself as a direct descendent of Solomon and morally bound to dispense that sovereign's level of justice. And his conquests were tenuous. A country that has been rife with tribal conflicts for generations does not soon settle down to single rule. There were members of Theodore's own family who threatened his peace.

Our image of John Bell toward the end of the 1850's is that of a man deeply committed to his sovereign and strongly content in his private life. Henry Stern gives us an affecting report of Bell's place in society and his home life. He writes of joining Bell in a journey to some hot water baths:

"Orders having already been communicated to a division of Mr. Bell's horse to accompany us, these faithful and attached warriors, glad to enjoy a short respite from ... battle, well mounted, and in a soldierlike attitude, awaited their respected general's appearance.... An hour's sharp ride beside the smooth waters of the Tzana, conducted us to a green dark-leafed forest glade, where, in the thickest shade, concealed from every profane gaze, Mrs. Bell – an Abyssinian lady of rank - ... awaited her spouse.... Several detachments of troops passed our hiding place, and, in anticipation of obtaining some news, ... they were inclined to intrude on our privacy; but on being told

that a woizero, or lady of rank, was near, they all hurried away from the forbidden ground." (12, p. 85)

After lingering awhile in the forest dell, the party moves forward.

On his way back to Debra Tabor, Stern turns aside to visit "... the nocturnal abode of the Anglo-Abyssinian noble". He is surprised to see the ubiquitous round hut of the country constructed of branches and roofed with grass. Stumbling over the doorway he hears a laughing voice calling, " 'Here is a hand, and if you object to the obnoxious fumes, a well-filled pipe is a sure antidote....' " (12, p 88) Stern grasps the extended hand and, so guided, lands on an alga (or couch). He remonstrates with Bell at sitting in smoke and dust when he might be out in the glorious air and sunshine. Bell revealingly declares," ' don't lecture me on the luxuries of dews and blue skies, to which I am condemned eight months out of every twelve....' " (12, p. 88) Stern yields, and listens to his friend's humorous comparison of the happy life of the savage compared to the woe incurred by those encompassed by the conventions of civilization. And then, in a little while,

"... the voices of servants, the neighing of horses, and the clank and clash of lance and sword reminded us that the time for our departure had arrived. A numerous assemblage of male and female attendants, together with several officers and the whole population of the straggling village... - [with] great deference and respect – awaited the appearance of the popular and beloved Lik-a-maquas. The reed door being pushed aside, all the civil and military authorities prostrated themselves on the unclean ground, and, in a hoarse chorus, bawled forth a whole string of morning salutations." (12, p. 89)

Truly, John Bell had found his element.

~

Early in 1860, Walter Plowden was pressed by the British Foreign Office to return to Massawa, on the coast. The Emperor warned him that the roads were unsafe, but in March Plowden set out as per his instructions. He was not very far from Gondar when he was met by Theodore's cousin, and deadliest enemy, Gared. It was Plowden's misfortune that Abyssinians were far more likely to connect him with Theodore than with the British government. Gared attacked, and Plowden's small retinue resisted, but Gared was able to thrust his lance into Plowden's chest. He was carried to Gondar where he died nine days later. One can still see his stone gravesite not far from the lovely Debre Berhan Salassie Church

Walter Plowden's death was a devastating loss for John Bell. They had been friends since they had met in Suez seventeen years before. They had shared adventure, hardship and the loneliness of self exile. Still, the work of the state went forward, and the Emperor's favored chamberlain continued with his duties. He and Theodore planned that the next year Bell would lead a delegation of Abyssinians to England to be introduced to Western civilization and to assimilate some of its culture. It would be his first trip home in more than twenty years.

In December of 1860, The Emperor Theodore had massed his army in the northern province of Tigre, pursuing a rebel chief named Niguse, one of Wube's relatives. He had been in ascendancy in the region for the last few years while Theodore had been engaged in Gojjam to the south. Niguse was supported by the abhorrent Gared. Theodore's faithful liqemekwas was with him at Waldaba when, going through a wood, they came upon Gared and his brother. Both rebels attacked with their spears to kill the Emperor, but Bell was prepared and shot Gared dead before he could throw his spear. Then he saw the other warrior in the act of tossing his spear at Theodore, and hurled his body forward to protect the sovereign. The spear struck John Bell in the forehead and killed him instantly. In the next moment Theodore cut down the assailant and then, in a passion of grief, threw himself upon his dead friend's body.

It does seem as if at that moment something shattered within the King. He had been known to be devious at times, and even in the early years there were documented instances of his cruelty. But on that day he persuaded more than 1,500 men to surrender and then murdered them in cold blood. Their bodies were left in piles for hyenas to scavenge. A month later Niguse's main army was routed. He and his brother were seized at the sacred city of Aksum where Theodore ordered that their right hands and left feet should be hacked off, and they were left to perish in the sight of their people. There were not quite eight years left to Theodore's reign, and they would be years increasingly filled with horror.

As for my family, my great, great grandmother, Worqenesh, Bell's wife, retired to her mountain home where, according to Henry Dufton who traveled there in 1863, "Mr. Bell's widow and …the family of which she forms a part, consisting of her mother and grandmother, and no end of brothers and sisters …" had returned to live. (7, p. 162) There she remained in a little village on the side of Mount Gunna, while her daughters, Susan and Mary, stayed within the European community at Gaffat. Auntie Fana never mentioned Worqenesh Asfaw Yilma after Bell's death, but I like to think of her safely back within the embrace of a large, and still influential, family.

Bibliography (Part I)

1. Armbruster, Stephana. <u>Life and History of John Bell and his Descendants.</u> Palma de Mallorca: 1966.
2. Baker, Samuel W. <u>Exploration of the Nile Tributaries of Abyssinia.</u> Hartford: O. D. Case and Co. San Francisco: Faneir Dewing and Co: 1868.
3. Bell, John G. "Extract from a Journal of Travels in Abyssinia." <u>Miscellanea Aegyptiaca.</u> (1892): 9-25.
4. Blanc, Henry. <u>A Narrative of Captivity in Abyssinia</u>. London: Frank Cass & Co. Ltd. 1970.
5. Brinton, John. "Wreck of the Tigris." <u>Saudi Aramco World</u> (1969): Vol. 20, No. 2.
6. Crawford, James. Letter of 15th March 1844 to the Royal Geographic Society concerning Mr. Bell's journey to Abyssinia. Transcript of RGC/CB3/180.
7. Dufton, Henry. <u>Narrative of a Journey Through Abyssinia In 1862-3</u>. London: Elibron Classics, 2005.
8. Pankhurst, Richard. <u>Economic History of Ethiopia 1800-1955.</u> Addis Ababa: Haile Sellassie I University Press. 1968.
9. Parkyns, Mansfield. <u>Life In Abyssinia.</u> London: Frank Cass & Co. Ltd. 1966.
10. Plowden, Walter Chichelle. <u>Travels in Abyssinia and the Galla Country</u>. Ed. By Trevor Chichelle Plowden. London: 1868.
11. Stanley, Henry M. <u>The Story of Two British Campaigns in Africa</u>. New York: Harper & Brothers, 1874.
12. Stern, Henry Arron. <u>Wandering Among the Falashas in Abyssinia</u>. London: Frank Cass & Co. Ltd. 1968.

PART II

MARY AND KARL

A thousand shall fall at thy side,
And ten thousand at thy right hand;
But it shall not come nigh thee.
         —Psalm 91:7

Travel Routes

Wega Miller George

My great grandmother, Mary Bell Saalmuller, was born in her parents' home in Diddim, in the province of Begemder, in 1853. She was still alive when I was born in 1936, so I was named for her as well as for my two grandmothers. She was the youngest of the three Bell children, and must have had a happy childhood. Her father was both honored and loved, and her mother's relatives were the most prominent family in the local area. Mary often recounted to her daughters memories of her early years – how on holy days the priests would bless the house and their neighbors would come with flowers and express their good wishes. Then the family would spread out a great meal for all to enjoy. Mary was only seven years old when her father was killed. Her elder sister had been married the year before, at the age of fifteen, to a Swiss missionary, Theophilus Waldmeier. From the time of her father's death, Abyssinia began to sink into turmoil and the people to suffer shortages and political terrors. In 1867, when she was only fourteen, Mary married Waldmeier's friend and colleague, Karl Saalmuller.

Saalmuller was a German who, when barely twenty, went out to Abyssinia as a lay missionary. I know nothing of his early life. From reading various sources I must deduce that he was a product of the Chrischona Institute near Basle, Switzerland; and had been recruited to work in Abyssinia by the then Protestant Bishop of Jerusalem, Samuel Gobat. I think of my great grandfather as an extremely practical and capable man who was, nevertheless, often overshadowed by the more dominant personality of his brother-in-law.

~

In the autumn of 1858, when Mary Bell was only five, Karl Saalmuller, Mr. and Mrs. Flad (also lay missionaries) and a Mr. Schroth and his son (sent as technical workmen) joined Theophilus Waldmeier in Alexandria, Egypt; and the little party proceeded up the Nile toward Abyssinia. It was to prove an arduous journey. From Alexandria the group was able to travel by train to Cairo where, fascinated by the land of the Pharaohs, they visited the pyramids of Giza, Cheops and Mycrena. Here the rails ended and they continued their journey south by boat, fighting the current of the river. They needed a strong wind to move the vessel along, so progress was slow and they had ample leisure to study the land. They traveled to Luxor and Karnak, and then visited Thebes where, in a tomb, they saw a picture of brick making and remembered the story of the Children of Israel in captivity. Stopping at Korosko they abandoned the river to cross the Nubian Desert by camel. After sixteen days, suffering from thirst and heat in the day and cold at night, they regained the river at a little village named Abu-Hamed. From here they continued by boat to Khartoum. Along this stretch of the Nile they saw hundreds of crocodiles and were fascinated to watch the open-mouthed monsters enjoying the services of little birds cleaning their teeth. The river was also replete with hippopotamuses that Waldmeier recorded in drawings.

From Khartoum they sailed on the Blue Nile, and then again mounted camels to travel southeast through desert and wilderness. The heat was intense – so much so that the land was cracked open – and there were wild animals, but their greater fear was of the tribal Nubians. They finally reached Matemma, a place notorious not only for its deadly heat but for a large slave market. Continuing on to the base of the Abyssinian mountains and the small town of Wachnee, they all fell ill except for Mrs. Flad, who struggled to nurse them as well as she could. The Schroths succumbed to the illness, but the rest of the group recovered and pushed on. (7, pp. 3-11)

Waldmeier described the trip through the Sudan in lugubrious tones of sickness and death, but eventually the little group began to climb into the mountains of Abyssinia. At 6,000 feet above the sea the air was fresh, there were flowers in abundance and clean water was plentiful. Grateful to have attained a healthy climate, they little knew that they were entering a country where they would lose their freedom and, finally, suffer the terror of imminent execution.

Saalmuller, Waldmeier and the Flads arrive in Abyssinia early in 1859 and were presented to King Theodore by John Bell. Kindly received, they were sent to the amba, Meqdela, where other missionaries, Mr. and Mrs. Rosenthal, Mr. Staiger and Mr. Brandeis, were already situated. The new arrivals immediately took up the laborious task of learning the native language, Amharic. Saalmuller and Waldmeier also spent time each day teaching mechanical skills to some of the Abyssinians, which appreciably raised them in the King's esteem.

Meqdela served as a safe fortress for King Theodore. Here he stored his treasure and the accumulation of gifts from other countries and here, too, he imprisoned his enemies. The amba was protected by a garrison of at least one thousand of his soldiers. Believing that the fortress was not a suitable mission station, the little group appealed to John Bell to intercede for them with the King to provide another location for their work. And so they were given a small area in the fertile plains and hills just east of Debra Tabor named Gaffat. They came to be known as the Gaffat people and Theodore called them his "Gaffat children."

The mission group left Meqdela in June of 1860 and arrived at Gaffat within a week. Waldmeier tells us that they built twelve small huts, "...each in five days, from small pieces of wood, covered with straw outside, and well plastered within. Each of us had two huts, one for dwelling and sleeping, the other for a kitchen." (7, p. 63) Gaffat became a little colony of Europeans, some of whom were missionaries, some artisans and some both; and a magnet to the local population. Karl Saalmuller and Waldmeier continued to teach mechanical arts, and so continued in great favor with the King. These still early years of Theodore's reign were the time of a burgeoning industrial revolution in the country.

King Theodore was intent upon unifying and reforming his country. Having spent his youth fighting border wars against Egypt, he recognized the necessity for modernizing his army, both in its structure and its weaponry. He saw the little community at Gaffat as a means for producing cannons and mortars to replace lances and spears. An early initiative that continued throughout his reign was the construction of decent roads to make possible the rapid repositioning of troops and supplies. Saalmuller and Waldmeier were appointed to supervise these enterprises. Workmen who came to Abyssinia from France and Germany were directed to Gaffat, among who were a gun maker and an iron founder worker. Samuel Baker, in his account of exploration along the Blue Nile, speaks of meeting "...two German missionaries...en route for an establishment that had been set...in the heart of Abyssinia.... One of these preachers was a blacksmith...." (2, p. 523) Theodore sent hundreds of his most capable countrymen to work in the Gaffat foundries where guns were cast and bored. A great water wheel was built for moving the different pieces of machinery. The remains of these industrial facilities exist to this day. The King was delighted with the activity, and would sit for hours in conversation with the missionaries. So pleased was he that he, the self-proclaimed Lion of Judah and the only person in Abyssinia permitted to keep lions, presented Waldmeier with a lion cub. The cub, that the missionary named Hagos, grew to an enormous size and his roar was so powerful, "... that he made the air tremble, as well as the cows, sheep, and goats, who were near him." (7, p. 77) Growing up in the midst of the mission group and well fed by the kind attentions of Theodore, Hagos was gentle enough that Waldmeier's little daughter, Rosa, could ride on his back while holding her father's hand. So for a very few years, until the end of 1863, the Europeans thrived. Theodore supported their mission and life at Gaffat was cheerful and productive.

~

But all the while there were undercurrents of trouble in the offing. There had been two principal influences for good in Theodore's life. His first wife, Tewabach, had devotedly loved and cared for him. As part of her care she had overseen his diet and diligently curtailed his consumption of alcohol. She had also been his good friend, reading and talking with him and creating an atmosphere of calm. John Bell, until his death in 1860, had been his trusted friend and administrator, offering wise counsel in matters of state. Now both were gone. Theodore began to drink and, while he never appeared intoxicated in public, even a moderate use of alcohol seemed to inflame his already excitable nature and to enable him to commit cruel and unjust acts. Finally, the English Consul who was sent to replace Walter Plowden at Theodore's court in 1862, Captain Charles Cameron, and his secretary, a Frenchman named Bardel, were never the equal of Plowden and Bell.

King Theodore received Cameron and Bardel with all due honor and indicated that he wished to improve his country's relationship with both England and France. Consequently, in November of 1862 he sent two letters – one to Queen Victoria and one to the Emperor Napoleon III – describing his jurisdiction and suggesting a diplomatic envoy to each country.

He charged both Cameron and Bardel that each deliver the letter in person to his respective sovereign.

Bardel and Cameron left Abyssinia for the port of Massawa on the Red Sea and, for a while, all was well. Bardel went by steamer directly to France, but Cameron sent Theodore's letter and his own cover letter by Foreign Office post and proceeded to an area in the Sudan that was in open rebellion against Theodore because of his opposition to the slave trade. Cameron expected to remain there until a letter from Earl Russell, of the Foreign Office, reached him to be conveyed back to Theodore, but no letter came. The letter from the King seemed to have been misplaced, and Cameron's cover letter was laid aside. When Russell finally communicated with Cameron, it was to the effect that England was not going to meddle in the internal affairs of Abyssinia. Cameron was obliged to return to Abyssinia empty-handed. The King was deeply disappointed and, when subsequently he learned that Cameron had been in the Sudan instead of London, he was livid. At the end of 1863 a letter arrived from Russell's office reminding Cameron that he was to leave Abyssinia for Massawa, where he was to serve as Consul. There was no longer to be a representative of the English government at Theodore's court at all. Theodore reasoned that the English were more interested in courting the Egyptians and their cotton than himself. He was not far off the mark: it was the time of the American Civil War. He forthwith cast Captain Cameron in chains and sent him off to the prison at Meqdela.

At about the same time, Theodore became aware of a book about travels in Abyssinia that had been published in England by an earlier missionary, Dr. Henry Stern. The Frenchman, Bardel, translated certain of its unflattering passages to the King, who was enraged. Theodore complained to Waldmeier that he had believed all Europeans to be as his beloved John Bell, but they were not - they were liars. Unaware of Theodore's anger, Dr. Stern returned to Abyssinia in 1863. At first, at the King's order, he was severally beaten and was sentenced to be executed, but in 1864, along with Mr. and Mrs. Rosenthal and their European servants, he was sent to the prison at Meqdela. Mr. and Mrs. Flad, Mr. Staiger and Mr. Brandeis were allowed to remain at Gaffat, but as semi-prisoners. The Waldmeiers and Karl Saalmuller remained ostensibly free, and Mary Bell, who was now eleven years old, continued as a member of the Waldmeier's household. But all of the Europeans were now suspect, and their daily existence was precarious.

~

At last the British government became alarmed when they learned of the imprisonment of their consul and of other Europeans, and sent one Hormuzd Rassam, accompanied by a Dr. Blanc (a medical doctor), to negotiate for their release. Interestingly, Rassam's name had appeared with John Bell's years earlier. There had been an Iraqi of that name on the 1836 expedition down the Euphrates River in which Bell had participated. He had served as an interpreter. I think it is likely that this was the same person.

In 1864 Rassam was the First Assistant Political Resident at the British consulate at Aden. In June of that year he suddenly received word that he should make ready to deliver a letter from Her Royal Majesty to the sovereign of Abyssinia. Because Consul Cameron had sent out word that his imprisonment was due to Theodore's extreme displeasure at never receiving an answer to his friendly overtures to the English Queen, the government now, belatedly, decided to send a courteous and conciliatory response. Rassam's instructions were, if possible, to deliver the letter himself, but on no account to further the imbroglio. Rassam had to wait until the 20th of July to receive the Queen's letter. On that same afternoon he and Henry Blanc embarked on the *Dalhousie* to sail across the Red Sea to the port of Massawa, a Turkish stronghold bordering on Abyssinia.

Three days later they sighted the coast of Africa. Sailing toward Massawa the two Englishmen were enchanted by the sight of the mountains of Abyssinia in the background and a seeming island paradise of green trees and white houses rapidly approaching. Their landing at Massawa quickly disabused them of any sense of delight. There were mangrove swamps, burning sand and squalid huts. The island, that was the jumping off place to the African mainland, was a coral reef with daytime temperatures well over 100 degrees Fahrenheit and evening readings only slightly lower. The heat and environment were debilitating, and it was here and in the surrounding countryside that the two men were delayed, at Theodore's pleasure, for fifteen months.

During the course of those long, uncomfortable months, Rassam wrote to the King on three separate occasions explaining his mission and requesting permission to enter the country. It was always difficult to engage reliable couriers, and the trip from Massawa to the royal court (often on the move) was fraught with bandits and rebellious tribes. A sortie and return could not be accomplished in less than two months, so Rassam and Blanc sat down to wait. Rassam came to believe that Theodore would not reply to his dispatches because Abyssinia was in turmoil and he was embarrassed that he could not guarantee a safe passage for the Englishmen. Others were sure that Theodore found pleasure in toying with the Englishmen. In the meantime the British Foreign Office augmented their Mission by adding a military officer, Lieutenant Prideaux, who joined them in May of 1865. It was hoped that this addition would somehow impress Theodore with the importance of the Mission, but as Henry Blanc noted, the only gain was in a, "…charming companion who was doomed to spend with me in a tent on the sea-beach the hot months of hot Massowah." (3, p. 77)

At long last the English Mission, now composed of Hormuzd Rassam, Henri Blanc and Lieutenant Prideaux, received a barely civil letter from King Theodore in response to Rassam's third request. It was neither signed nor sealed, but it did give the Mission permission to attend upon his court. However, they were not to take the direct route from Massawa to Debra Tabor, but rather must trace a circuitous path along the northern border of Abyssinia through Sudan in order to enter the country by way of the western border city of Matemma. Once they arrived at Matemma they were directed to notify Theodore so that he might send them an escort to bring them to his court. On the afternoon of the 15th of October, 1865, the Mission composed of Rassam (carrying the Queen's letter), Dr. Blanc and Lieutenant Prideaux, along with an escort provided by the local Turkish Pasha, several servants and muleteers, and with forty-five heavily laden camels, began their tortuous journey to the court of King Theodore. They hurried away from Massawa in the midst of a cholera epidemic.

The journey inland took them six weeks and was accomplished with little difficulty. Rassam, Blanc and Prideaux cantered into Matemma on their mules on the afternoon of the 21st of November, with their entourage following in the late evening. They heard, on their arrival, that Theodore was at Gondar, only five days distant, and immediately sent word of their arrival hoping that the King would summon them at once. A month passed, and then a dismal Christmas, but on the next day Rassam received two letters from Theodore. Again, one lacked both seal and signature; but the second, written three days later, was the epitome of gracious expression. Rassam was addressed as "dear one", and Theodore had sent orders to three local chiefs to receive the Mission and to escort it to the royal court. On the afternoon of the 28th, Rassam, Blanc and Prideaux finally crossed the border into Abyssinia and began their trek into the Highlands. (5, p. 180)

It took exactly a month for the English Mission to attain the royal court, which it finally intercepted on the plains of Gojjam near Damot. The little group of three with its few servants and laden camels had swelled to at least 1,200 as Theodore's call for chiefs and their retainers swept the countryside. On the 28th of January, 1866, in sight of the royal tents, Rassam, Blanc and Prideaux began their final approach to the royal presence. Henry Blanc described the striking pageantry:

In the valley between the hills a large body of cavalry, about 10,000 strong, formed a double line, between which we advanced. On our right, dressed in gorgeous array, almost all bearing the silver shield and the Bitwa, their horses adorned with richly plated bridles, stood the whole of the officers of his Majesty's army and household. All were mounted, some on really noble-looking animals, tribute from the plateaus of Yedjow and the highlands of Shoa. On our left, the corps of Cavalry was darker, but more compact, than it's aristocratic vis-à-vis...We advanced slowly towards the beautiful durbar-tent of red and yellow silk, between a double line of gunners, who, on a signal, fired a salute....(3, pp. 126-8)

Upon entering the tent they found the King sitting on a sofa and dressed in a shamma (a common wrap of the country, often with a wide red stripe on one side) with which he had wound himself up almost to his eyes. Pleasantries were exchanged, and gradually the shamma slipped down. This first meeting was replete with court etiquette and kindliness to the weary travelers. The King graciously greeted the representatives of the British Queen and kindly inquired as to their health and well-being.

He assigned Ayto Samuel as Rassam's balderaba, or facilitator, between the mission and the court. He also declared himself satisfied with the Queen's letter and grateful for Rassam's tenacity in delivering it. Even so, he found opportunity to broach such subjects as Captain Cameron's officious behavior, Dr. Stern's duplicity, the quite irrelevant subject of the supposed treachery of the Abune Salama (the head of the Abyssinian church) and the perverse conduct of his own subjects, whom he described as 'a wicked people'. (5, p. 250) So began a most delicately balanced friendship. The King always declared Rassam his friend; and Rassam, now a witness to Theodore's wide-ranging harangues, always treated the King with firmness, tempered with grace. Rassam tells us that he could never match Theodore in the effusion of his courtly address, but he did seem to come close.

Here, at the very outset of the relationship between Rassam and the King, there may have been a basic misunderstanding. The letter to Theodore from the Queen was delivered in the original English. On this particular occasion there was no one at hand to make the translation directly into Amharic and so it was first rendered into Arabic and then Amharic. (5, pp. 254-5) It is no wonder that this resulted in shadings of innuendo so as to obfuscate meaning. A sentence recommending Rassam to Theodore as having the full trust of Her Majesty was interpreted by the King to say that Rassam was a most trustworthy gentleman who would do anything the King might ask of him! (7, p. 87)

In any case, there were now three distinct groups of Europeans in Abyssinia who would interact with each other and impact the life of Mary Bell, who had reached the age of thirteen. First, there were those imprisoned at amba Meqdela including Consul Cameron, Dr. Stern and the Rosenthals. Second were the missionaries and artisans, such as Karl Saalmuller and Theophilus Waldmeier, who had been allowed to continue their work at Gaffat. And now, in addition to these two groups, there was the English Mission consisting of Hormuzd Rassam, Dr. Henry Blanc and Lieutenant Prideaux.

~

On the day following their first meeting, the King indicated to Rassam that he would immediately release Consul Cameron and the Rosenthals into his custody. On the 3rd of February Theodore finally directed an officer to go to Meqdela, release the prisoners from their chains and bring them to Rassam; but within hours he reversed the order, excusing himself by saying he had not yet fixed on a meeting place. On the 5th Theodore directed the English mission to go to Korata (on the shores of Lake Tsana) and await the prisoners there, but still he did not send the order for their release. If ever there was a frustrating assignment demanding unlimited quantities of forbearance, surely it was that of Hormuzd Rassam. The Mission, as directed by the King, left for Korata on the 14th, crossing Lake Tsana in local canoes (tanquas) built of papyrus reeds, that assured a thorough drenching. By this time the king had finally sent officers to remove Consul Cameron's chains and escort him, with the other European prisoners, to Rassam.

Their early days in Korata were probably the happiest that the three members of the English Mission spent in Abyssinia. Korata was a center of both trade and religion, and the streets were crowded with well-to-do merchants and priests of the Abyssinian Church. The Englishmen, at the orders of the King, were themselves treated like royalty. Shunning occupancy of vermin-ridden houses in the city, they pitched their tents on the sandy shores of Lake Tsana, relishing the fresh air and clean water. To assure their comfort, Theodore ordered his "Gaffat children" to join them and keep them company. Initially, Rassam, Blanc and Prideaux were startled by the Abyssinian dress and demeanor of these European missionaries and artisans, but soon came to recognize their education and intelligence. In particular they identified Theophilus Waldmeier and Karl Saalmuller as men of integrity whom they could rely upon. The Europeans were joined by their wives and families. Susan Bell Waldmeier and her young sister, Mary, came to tea, dressed in gorgeous Abyssinian costume. They had to converse through an interpreter as, at that time, the two spoke only Amharic. Shortly after the appearance of the Europeans from Gaffat, Consul Cameron and the Europeans who had been imprisoned arrived in Korata. In theory, they were now placed under the authority of Hormuzd Rassam.

It was the 12th of March, 1866, when, looking much the worse for wear, the Europeans who had been held at Meqdela joined the English mission. There were thirteen adults including Consul Cameron, M. Bardel, Dr. Stern and Mr. and Mrs. Rosenthal. Rassam greeted them cordially, but was afraid to show too much pleasure in seeing them for fear of offending the King. Theodore's direction to him was, in his stead, to conduct a trial of the offenders. If it seemed that they were innocent of misconduct toward the King, he would "requite" them; but if indeed they had abused the King, they should provide indemnity to him, or, to be more specific, substantial damages. When the letter containing Theodore's charges arrived, to be read to the former prisoners in front of the Mission, the Gaffat people and various Abyssinian officials, they were specific only against Cameron and Bardel and vaguely general against the others. Of course, all acknowledged their guilt and begged for pardon and absolution. The proceedings were a farce. (6, pp. 34-36)

Correspondence with the King ensued and, gradually, it became apparent that while Theodore might pardon the prisoners, he was at the same time most anxious for the English Queen to send skilled workers to Abyssinia to teach his people the arts of ship-building and gun-making. The two groups where intertwined in his mind. While the prisoners might leave the country under the escort of Dr. Blanc and Lieutenant Prideaux, he intended his dear friend, Hormuzd Rassam, to stay by his side until the skilled workers from England should arrive. Rassam argued that he could better represent the King's needs if he presented them to the Queen in person. He had always understood his mission to be simply the release and recovery of the imprisoned Europeans. Theodore, who had really formed an attachment for Rassam, hoped to retain his services for as long as possible.

The Royal Court, now having depleted the resources of a large part of the area of Metcha to the south of Lake Tsana, moved to encamp on the Zege peninsula, a piece of land that juts three miles into the Lake near its southeast corner. Its location was about ten miles south of Korata: in fact, the Mission could see the smoke rising from the royal kitchen fires.

Two weeks after the arrival of the Meqdela prisoners in Korata, the English Mission, accompanied by eight Europeans from Gaffat, traveled by tanqua to Zege. As usual with such travel, they were drenched. When dry and changed, they were met by Ras Ingida, King Theodore's prime minister, and given richly-furnished mules to ride from the beach to the royal camp. Here they were provided with new silk tents and a plentiful supply of foodstuff. Instead of waiting for them to attend upon him, Theodore appeared at their tents. In an unparalleled show of respect, he took his right arm from his robe and greeted Rassam. Conversing there for ten minutes, he then particularly invited the English Mission to come along with him for a chat. The King took Rassam by the hand and they walked together to an audience hall followed by Blanc and Prideaux, and further back by Waldmeier, Saalmuller and the other European artisans. For the next two hours the King chatted pleasantly, introducing one of his sons, displaying weapons and conversing on a variety of topics. Again, he could not resist bringing up his antipathy for Consul Cameron, Dr. Stern and the Abune Salama; but the atmosphere was calm and friendly. Waldmeier noted that no one could handle King Theodore as could Hormuzd Rassam, and it appeared to be so. (7, p. 88)

By the next morning the feeling in the camp had changed. Theodore had summoned his Chiefs, and the topic for consideration was now whether or not the former European prisoners should be allowed to leave at all. Again, the Gaffat people were ordered to appear. Witnesses reported to Rassam that, "First he [the King] consulted Ayto Samuel [Rassam's balderaba] and Wald-Gabir, the valet and constant attendant on the King, and when they advised him to send me to my country with joy, he told them that they were asses and blockheads, and did not know what they were saying." (5, pp. 58-9) Next, he addressed the Gaffat group who advised him that he needed no surety, but could implicitly trust the English Queen's word that she would send workmen. Theodore asked them to wait outside. Now there were only the Chiefs to consult. When the King asked them if he should not retain Rassam as a guarantee that the Queen would favorably respond to his petition, they were unanimous in advising the King to let him go. Theodore was stymied, but not forestalled. When he had dismissed all of his advisors the King had Ras Ingida send for Rassam, who reappeared at the audience hall with his companions. Waldmeier and Saalmuller were summoned back as well.

Rassam entered the hall and saw immediately that the King was in a foul mood. Theodore told Rassam that all whom he had consulted advised him to let Rassam go, and he spent the next two hours castigating a long list of persons who had entered his country and then rewarded his hospitality with ingratitude. Why should he expect otherwise from Rassam? Even if Rassam did not abuse him, he would forget him. Rassam could only ask Theodore for his trust, and finally he acquiesced. The understanding was that Rassam should return to Korata, organize all of the Europeans who wished to leave the country and be ready to depart soon after Easter. The King asked that Rassam visit him one more time before he left. The weather was threatening; but Rassam, knowing the King's mood, refused to delay crossing back to Korata. As Ras Ingida escorted him to the sieve-like boats on the beach, he noted quietly that on Rassam's next leave-taking he hoped to escort him farther. Rassam truly believed that the prime minister sincerely wished for his safe exit from the country. (6, p. 65)

~

From the time that Rassam returned to Korata, there seemed to be tension and trouble in the air. It was rumored that the Gaffat people had been asked to corroborate for the former Meqdela prisoners, the dates and details of their suffering, but Waldmeier assured Rassam that they had refused to comply. Documentation of this sort would have enraged the King and brought danger to all. Flowery letters continued to pass daily between Zege and Korata, and Rassam received assurances from Theodore that their departure was expected and approved. The 1st of April was Easter for the Western Church, and all of the Protestant community gathered in Rassam's tent to worship. Dr. Stern celebrated Holy Communion, and the service was followed by a large meal with all of the European artisans and their wives. Susan Waldmeier and Mary Bell helped Rassam to entertain the gathering. There were so many present, that dinner had to be served from the floor. (6, p.70)

The days passed with a continuous stream of letters, Theodore writing of his joy at the approach of Easter which, for the Abyssinian Church, took place on the 8th. On that same day Rassam received an oral communication from the King, delivered by Ayto Samuel, that the released prisoners should soon proceed to the northeast corner of Lake Tsana under the escort of Henry Blanc and Lieutenant Prideaux to await Rassam's leave-taking of Theodore. Within hours this plan was set aside and the Mission heard of a newly-constructed enclosure in the King's camp. None knew its purpose. Rassam now sent a specific letter to the King requesting that the former captives might travel around the eastern shore of the Lake and then on to

Matemma to wait for him to join them. It had always been his certain belief that these long-suffering souls should not be paraded in front of the King on their departure. Rassam was convinced that the sight of Consul Cameron and Dr. Stern would send Theodore into a frenzy. On the 10th he received a reply stating that the King approved this proposal. All seemed well.

On the morning of the 12th, it was reported that the King had not slept during the night and that he was in a dreadful mood. He gave orders that the released captives should be allowed to leave Korata and head north, but that they should be intercepted at a little village about a day's march away and returned, in chains, to Zege.

The next morning the unwitting former captives began their trek northward. Rassam, accompanied by Henry Blanc, Lieutenant Prideaux and the Gaffat artisans, once again boarded local tanquas and began another damp ride to Zege. And once again Rassam, Blanc and Prideaux were met by Ras Ingida, ordered to change into their government uniforms and presented with royal mules to ride to Theodore's camp.

Upon arriving, the English Mission immediately noticed that this time there were no gaily colored tents to accommodate them. When they reached the audience hall, followed by Saalmuller and Waldmeier, they saw that it was packed with ranking Chiefs. They next looked toward the throne, and it was empty. Stepping forward, they were suddenly each seized by three sturdy Chiefs, manhandled and their clothes torn. The assault happened so quickly that Rassam thought somehow they had missed seeing the King and had failed to salute him. Ras Ingida looked back to tell them not to be afraid, and Rassam finally realized that they were under arrest. The King, all the while, was sitting behind a door, listening. (6, pp. 82-3)

A period of interrogation ensued, and the questions, conveyed from the King, were all superficial and staged. Rassam's answers were dignified and direct, earning the approval of the assembled Chiefs. As usual, the King's royal lineage was recited. At last he seemed to become calmer and somewhat apologetic, but still announced that the former prisoners had been recaptured and were on their way to Zege. When they arrived he, the King, would decide what he should do. In the meantime Rassam, Blanc and Prideaux were given a tent near the King, but were held under heavy guard. No one was allowed to go near them, not even Waldmeier and Saalmuller. The men who had come to Abyssinia to free the European prisoners were now themselves imprisoned.

In the meantime Consul Cameron and his party had been taken back to Korata, where they learned of the arrest of their would-be rescuers. Here they were kindly cared for by the wives of the Gaffat artisans who were now in dread for the lives of their men folk. Susan Waldmeier had had no word from Theophilus, and her sister, Mary, was anxious for Karl Saalmuller, whom she was beginning to think of as a special friend and protector.

By the 15th of April, Cameron and the others arrived at Zege and were placed apart from the Mission in the newly-constructed enclosure. It was now apparent that the whole ruse had been carefully planned, at least for some days. Cameron and his fellows were to be tried yet again. On the following morning the country's foremost Chiefs were assembled to the court in which the King intended to question the prisoners. The members of the Mission were told to don their formal uniforms and attend as "friends" of the King, and the European artisans were ordered to stand behind them. The King, speaking in a placating manner, insisted to Rassam that he never meant his men to handle Rassam and his colleagues roughly, and complained that they should not have worn their dress swords. It was Theodore's usual pattern of dredging up extraneous excuses for his abominable behavior. In a short while Consul Cameron and the other prisoners appeared, chained two by two.

There followed another farcical trial. Rassam found himself taking full blame for having allowed the former prisoners to approach the border of the country without first going to the King to be reconciled with him, and beg for his pardon. Denied that, Rassam promised to act as their guarantor so that they might be released from their fetters. It was another twenty-four hours before even this boon was granted. The whole affair was rigged. A smile played on Theodore's face as he accused Rassam of trying to smuggle the prisoners out of the country.

In the end, the King determined to write a letter to the English Queen. In it he claimed to have freed Cameron and the other European prisoners and to have turned them over to Hormuzd Rassam. He was keeping Rassam with him to consult with him and to continue their friendship. He then had Rassam write a companion letter requesting the Queen to send him various weapons, and persons with technical skills. Mr. Flad was chosen to carry the letters, being forced to leave his wife and three children behind. In effect, Rassam was to be a hostage until the fulfillment of the King's requests. There was no one to stop the charade. Those Abyssinian Chiefs who admired Rassam could do nothing to help him. Waldmeier and Saalmuller stood by in horror.

Through the end of the month Theodore continued the pretense of friendship for Rassam and of kindly concern for the other Europeans. He consulted them on ship building and took Rassam and his companions duck hunting. One day they went to shoot hippopotamuses off the southern tip of the Zege peninsula, and another they were invited to watch the King and his Chiefs play the national game of guks. Rassam, though he marveled at the King's grace and agility jousting on horseback, could only deplore his mental instability. The man who had come to power through a genius for military campaign was ruining his country through caprice. Theodore encouraged Rassam, Blanc and Prideaux to ride each day for exercise and enjoyment, but often when they left the camp the King would conduct cruel floggings and executions among his own people. Poor Mrs. Rosenthal's tent was closest to the spot where these horrors occurred, and she could hear the lashes descending on the bodies of the victims. The Theodore who had been all gracious smiles and kindly concern was now revealed as a murderous despot. To add to everyone's misery, the rainy season began in mid May, and by the end of the month Zege had become mired in mud and unhealthy with fever. The King had planned to relocate his camp to the higher country toward Debra Tabor, but before he made his move there was an outbreak of cholera and typhus. On the evening of May 31, the English Mission and the Rosenthals (Mrs. Rosenthal was pregnant) were sent across Lake Tsana to Korata on their way to the new camp. There was a gale blowing, forcing the little boats to make frequent stops along the shore. Without doubt, this was their wettest and most harrowing crossing yet.

  The trip to Debra Tabor was even more dreadful for the remainder of the Europeans including the Waldmeiers, Mary Bell, and Karl Saalmuller. Rather than being sent by ship, they were forced to join the King's army, rounding the south east corner of Lake Tsana by land. As the rains continued, the thousands marching turned the ground to mire. The crowd contained not only soldiers, but their wives and children. Many were sick and dying – some carried by their families and others dropped to the earth and trampled by the crowd. Grief surrounded them, and the stench of disease and death was overwhelming. It took days to reach Debra Tabor. By the time the little group of artisans took their leave of Theodore's forces and pushed on to Gaffat, Susan Waldmeier was desperately sick with cholera. Theophilus raced back on the little footpath between Gaffat and Debra Tabor to beg the King to allow Dr. Blanc to go with him to Gaffat that he might attend Susan. Theodore, remembering his first wife, Tewabach, with tears in his eyes hastened to agree. It was one of the few instances of a humane gesture, on his part, during these dreadful days following Rassam's arrest. Mary and Theophilus nursed Susan and she began to recover, only to be struck down again, this time by typhus. Somehow, she survived. (7, pp. 89-90)

During those rainy days of June the English mission was sent to Gaffat to be housed, first in the artisans' homes and then at the foundry; but on the 25th, Rassam and his companions were hastily summoned to Debra Tabor to appear at court. At first they assumed that there was a rebel chief to be tried, but quickly learned that it was Rassam himself who was called on the carpet. The King had received information about a railway that was said to be under construction in the Sudan by the French and English, supposedly preparatory to an invasion of Abyssinia. Surely Rassam must have seen this project on his way through Sudan to Matemma, yet he had not mentioned it to the King. How could he claim the King's friendship and not have warned him? Secondly, Theodore asserted that he had heard from sources in Jerusalem that Rassam had been sent by his government to release and recover the captives so that Britain might then revenge herself of insult by invading the country. Rassam hastened to argue the impossibility of both charges and to insist that his government did not behave with such duplicity. Both accusations had been trumped up by trouble makers, but the King continued to be uneasy. Now, here was a second disgrace for Rassam and the Mission. (6, pp. 140-2)

So the King acted to remove the English Mission from the comparative comfort and freedom in Gaffat to close confinement in the King's camp. The house used for their imprisonment was built of stone and had only a single door, with no window or other opening. Their only light was from candles, and it did not take much imagination to remind these three Englishmen of the black hole of Calcutta. Rassam complained bitterly to the King about this unfair treatment, and that evening Theodore exhibited his customary remorseful behavior, insisting upon visiting the prisoners, throwing their guards out of the house and sitting and drinking arrack and tej (a native drink made of fermented honey) with them. He remained for an hour or more, speaking calmly and charging himself with madness. (3, pp.177-8) This was the last time Rassam and his companions spoke directly with the King until twenty-one months later, when the British army was poised to attack Meqdela.

After the King's penitential visit the mission spent two more days huddled together in their black hole worrying about the King's intentions. It was with great relief that they heard they would soon be on the move. At first it seemed that they would spend the rainy season in Gaffat, but on the 5th of July they were told that Theodore was already on the road and that their escort was at hand. Delighted with the thought of fresh air and exercise, they were pleased to be in motion. They were joined by five of the former prisoners including Consul Cameron, Dr. Stern and Mr. Rosenthal. Mrs. Rosenthal was left behind in Gaffat in the care of Mrs. Flad. It was not long before they perceived that their general direction was continuously toward the southeast in a direct line to the amba, Meqdela. Theodore was variously pleasant toward them while he shared their road, sending Ayto Samuel to them to point out a large pile of hailstones or to take them to a vantage point to better view snow-covered mountains. On the 9th of July Theodore veered from their route, and in a few more days they were ceremoniously counted in to the confines of the prison at Meqdela. Within the week the chiefs in charge of the prison decided that it was better to err on the side of caution, and ordered leg chains for the new prisoners. They remained incarcerated and fettered until April of 1868. But if the deprivation of freedom and the loss of comfort and company were difficult, their existence at Meqdela was far easier and secure than that of their fellow Europeans who remained behind.

Life for the missionaries and artisans who were left at Gaffat became daily more toilsome and terrifying.

~

When Theodore turned aside from the road to Meqdela, he headed back to Debra Tabor with the intention of consolidating his position in the country, but Theodore was no longer the young, courteous campaigner who drew men to him by his courage and military genius, and he was no longer the just ruler of an adoring people. Returning to Begemder, the province in which Debra Tabor was situated, he began to bleed it dry. He had boasted that he would accomplish great things during the rainy season. Instead, he began to collect the annual tribute that was due from the local people. Not satisfied, he then insisted on advances on the next year's tribute. When, at length, the local chiefs could gather no more, Theodore became threatening and imprisoned them. Next, he looked further abroad and turned his attention to the riches of the mercantile interests and the churches of the old capital, Gondar. In early December, taking the elite of his army, he marched eighty miles in sixteen hours hoping to surprise the city, but by now his citizens were alert to his every move and the people of Gondar were warned. Many escaped, but the King searched and ravaged most of the city's buildings, including many of its churches. Fire spread from one structure to another, and those priests who stood about in anger were, themselves, cast into the flames. In an act of insane brutality, Theodore gathered up a group of young girls who had welcomed his entrance. Had their ululations warned those who had escaped? They were herded together and burnt alive. The King, who had once shown so much promise, had become a maniacal despot.

In March of the next year Theodore marched his army toward Korata to try to fill his treasury once more, but this time he failed. The people had been warned and they had packed up their goods on their tanquas and taken them across the Lake. Revenge was no longer easy. The soldiers of Theodore's army had begun to desert, and he was warned that these desertions would become massive if he destroyed Korata.

It was in this atmosphere that the Europeans in Gaffat were learning to cope. Five of them tried to escape, but were betrayed by the Frenchman, Bardel, and put in chains. Because of their offense some of their native friends were killed and others were stripped, tied with ropes and confined. All of the European artisans were now in danger every hour of every day.

In mid-April, 1867, Theodore sent soldiers to Theophilus Waldmeier's house, accusing him of duplicitous correspondence with England. Then all of the artisans' houses were surrounded, and Waldmeier and Karl Saalmuller were roughly dragged off to Debra Tabor. When Susan Waldmeier tried to follow she was thrown to the ground. Mary Bell huddled out of the way with her little niece, Rosa. The next day Waldmeier and Saalmuller were sent back along the path to Gaffat. They were told to hand over all of their property – clothes, books, money and furniture. The young Abyssinian who had been given charge of the boys school the Europeans had founded was called before the King, and his hands and feet were cut off. He lived, denied any assistance, for two more days. Late on that same evening the artisans, with their families, were escorted back to Debra Tabor. They had given up all of their possessions. In her anger, Susan Waldmeier had grabbed a golden saddle that the King had presented to her husband in happier times and hurled it out of an upstairs window. Mary saw it hit the head of one of the ubiquitous soldiers. (3, pp.91-2) This was the end of the six-year mission station at Gaffat. The halcyon days of lion cubs and happy chats with the King were quite over. Hagos had been shot, and his pelt given to a tribal chief. Now the challenge was to survive.

~

It is very strange to think, but it very well may be, that an oversized canon was responsible for keeping the European artisans alive. Of course, their individual acts of courage and their intelligence were contributive, but because King Theodore needed their expertise to first build, and then to transport this canon, he could not do without them.

Not long after they had been moved to Debra Tabor, Theodore came to Waldmeier and Saalmuller, returned their hand tools and a few of their possessions and told them that he needed a gun that would discharge a ball weighing 1,000 pounds. He cautioned them that he knew they had skills they did not speak of and that if they objected, claiming a lack of knowledge, he would know they were liars. Sure that if they refused the King he would kill them immediately, and if they failed their death would only have been postponed, the artisans could only say that they would try. The King was, for the moment, satisfied.

Waldmeier and Saalmuller put their heads together to design a mammoth canon. It was Karl Saalmuller who had the more technical skills along with another of the Gaffat artisans – a Pole named Moritz Hall who actually had experience of casting bells. They helped Waldmeier draw a design and then build a model which they presented to the King. With Theodore's approval they built two furnaces at Debra Tabor in preparation for casting the enormous weapon. The King brought hundreds of his people to be on hand to assist in the effort. The first casting failed. Saalmuller determined that unwanted moisture had entered the process, and the King resolved to try again. He was everywhere, taking hold of Waldmeier's hand and demanding how he might instruct his people. On the second attempt Waldmeier, "…asked the King to give the orders to open the channel of the furnace, and the heated brass ran like a fiery serpent into the larger mould prepared for it". (7, p. 94) Allowing the metal to cool, Waldmeier and Saalmuller waited three days and then opened the mould. With profound relief they found that the gun was sound. Theodore christened it, Sebastopol.

So, while the furnaces blazed to build weapons to fight the British, they were safe. It must have been at about this time, in the summer of 1867, that Karl Saalmuller married Mary Bell. Mary was probably still just fourteen, and Karl perhaps ten years older. Thrown together under the most awful conditions, the two had come to rely on each other, and their trust had engendered affection, and then love. To everyone's dismay Theodore insisted upon acting for Mary's father, his beloved, former chamberlain, and gave the bride away. He also provided a handsome wedding cloak richly embroidered in gold, and with a solid gold clasp in the front. This hiatus for familial concerns could not continue for very long.

There were brief respites of security when the King left Debra Tabor to go rampaging in the countryside. Then murmurings began among the Chiefs to kill the Europeans, but that was not practicable. The King had assigned them to build a wagon strong enough to carry the oversized cannon, Sebastopol. When the wagon was finished there were roads wanted to carry the heavy equipment. The Abyssinians needed both plans for the roads and oversight for their construction. They could not afford to rid themselves of the little band of artisans.

By now Mr. Flad had returned from his errand to England, carrying the Queen's reply to Theodore's prevarications and his request for skilled workmen. In addition to the formal letter, Flad had an oral message from Victoria. If Theodore did not release the prisoners at once, their friendship was at an end. Henry Blanc tells us that the King sat and listened to Mr. Flad and then said, "I have asked them for a sign of friendship, but it is refused me. If they wish to come and fight, let them, and call me a woman if I do not beat them." (3, p. 325)

The King continued with dreadful cruelty toward his own people. The killings were horrible. Some captives were shot, some burnt alive and still others were hanged. There was the dreadful torture of cutting off hands and feet leaving the victim to die without succor. Waldmeier remembered one awful execution when a group of three hundred victims was deliberately starved to death. (7, p. 95) The European artisans, acutely aware of the atrocities surrounding them, had been instructed to build two roads. With his usual military cunning, Theodore ordered one road in an easterly direction toward Meqdela and a second toward the south, and Gojjam. He did not intend to allow anyone to be sure of his plans.

~

The English government had, at last, heard of the imprisonment of its Mission and the re-imprisonment of the former captives including Consul Cameron, and had determined to send a military expedition to set all of the Europeans free. Theodore heard of its arrival on the coast of the Red Sea just south of Massawa and resolved to meet it at Meqdela. It was on the 1st of October, 1867, that Theodore began his drive to the east with all of his army and its heavy equipment in tow. The artisans toiled like slaves. Karl Saalmuller remembered the picture of the brick makers on the wall of the Egyptian tomb that he had seen on his journey into Abyssinia, and likened themselves to the children of Israel under Pharaoh. Meqdela is approximately 100 miles to the southeast of Debra Tabor, and it took Theodore's army six months to drag their artillery there. They had to blast rock, fill in ravines, cross mountains and forge rivers, building a road as they went. It was an amazing feat, and Theodore was everywhere – directing, encouraging, laboring and (when he was frustrated) killing.

What was now a little family group of Waldmeiers and

Saalmullers drew close together. The two men provided engineering and oversight for the trek across the highlands while Susan and Mary cared for little Rosa and provided hearth and home. Certainly, Waldmeier was no longer trusted by the King, although he could occasionally, by virtue of his indispensable, practical skills, nudge him away from violence. He richly described a typical scene of road building near Beit Hor that took place early in the next year:

After much trouble the King arrived with his camp at Beit Hor, on the edge of an immense gorge, 3000 feet deep, and 7 miles wide. This stupendous wall of rock is on the edge of the [D]alanta Highlands, and forms one side of the deep gorge in which the Tshitta river is hidden.... I had to act as engineer, and plan the road down to the bottom of this gorge and up on the other side of the height of [D]alanta. The other missionaries helped, and it was made, under our superintendence by thousands of men. After a short time the artillery and the whole camp passed safely across the plateau. (7, pp. 98, 101)

It was here that Waldmeier mustered the temerity to suggest to the King that he should send a message of reconciliation to Robert Napier, the commander of the approaching British expedition, to the effect that he would free the European prisoners. Enraged, the King aimed his pistol at the young man, but it misfired. Reaching to his side he next threw his spear which, narrowly missing Waldmeier's body, fell deeply into the ground at his side. Theodore's wrath subsiding, he imprisoned Waldmeier, but remembering his dependence on the artisan's expertise, instead ordered Waldmeier's tent to be moved close to his own.

Theodore's army was now almost visible to Rassam and his companions from the heights of Meqdela, yet it was still nearly three months' distant. From Beit Hor the King sent on a number of Abyssinian prisoners and five Europeans to the confines of the amba, and breathed a sigh of relief when their safe arrival was acknowledged by the garrison's guns. He could see the smoke from their volley from the heights of a hill where he had retired to await this confirmation. The land between Beit Hor and Meqdela was filled with rebels, and he had feared for their safe passage. Now he worked to reconcile the people of Delanta (the province next to Meqdela) to himself that he might access both their food and their labor. Successful in claiming their loyalty, the road building continued. There was still a 4,000 foot decline down to the Bashilo River (a tributary of the Blue Nile) to be built, and then on the other side of the river the long incline up to fortress Meqdela. The King was acutely aware of the English force drawing nearer every day, and the least breach of his equanimity would bring on cruel executions. Waldmeier and Saalmuller were frequently reminded that their turn could come at any moment. They were prepared to die, yet drew strength and hope from their little family group.

~

By the 4th of March, 1868, the royal camp had achieved the descent to the Bashilo and the King sent a message to Rassam to keep up his spirits as they would soon meet. The messenger had taken only four hours in transit. Word had also reached Rassam that the British expedition had progressed as far as the Takeze River, not more than twenty miles to the north. The opposing forces were about to converge near the heights of Meqdela. The flat-topped mountain rose from the plains above the Bashilo River. It was connected to a mountain peak, Salassie, by an elevated plateau known as Islamgee that extended to a third height, Fahla. This was the setting on which Theodore proposed to defend himself against, and even vanquish, the invaders. In quiet moments he would tell Waldmeier and Saalmuller that he longed for the day when he would look upon an organized, disciplined European army.

On the 16th, the King sent a message to his people on Meqdela that he was approaching. Rassam was advised to write to congratulate Theodore on his remarkable engineering achievement, and was rewarded with an order to the prison Chiefs to remove his chains. Rassam almost refused, out of loyalty to his companions who had not been given a similar release, but he was advised to accept. It was never wise to thwart the despot. By the evening of the 25th the King pitched his tent on the plateau of Islamgee. He had brought his artillery to the bottom of the up cropping and was hard at work on the final ascent.

The 29th of March was the day that the English mission first saw King Theodore after having been sent away from him twenty-one months earlier. They were each quite anxious at the prospect of facing the monarch, but as Rassam approached his tent, the King came out with his arm extended to shake his hand. Upon receiving Rassam's promise of surety for Dr. Blanc and Lieutenant Prideaux, Theodore ordered their chains removed as well. Dr. Blanc described how at first they could barely walk. Their legs seemed to be "…as light as feathers; we could not guide them, and we staggered very much like drunken men…." (3, p. 369) Theodore was calm and courteous during the meeting, assuring the men there was nothing to fear and that he would protect them during the coming conflict. That night, for the first time in many months, they slept unguarded.

With the British army drawing ever nearer, many of the Abyssinian soldiers became hostile to all of the Europeans, believing them to be responsible for the approaching danger. During the next few days one after another of them counseled the King to kill all of the foreigners. Theodore had other plans. The five Europeans who had just recently arrived at the amba were drafted to work on the road up the side of Islamgee: in return, their chains were removed. But in spite of their recent gentler treatment, none of the Europeans could be optimistic. All were too aware of Theodore's sudden mood changes and his propensity for violence. Their only comfort was their knowledge that the status quo was about to change. It was better to be killed than to continue longer in doubt and fear.

A few days later the King sent to the English Mission to attend him immediately. These summons were always unnerving – was there to be a polite conversation, chains or something worse? Nevertheless, having no choice, the three Englishmen donned their official uniforms and rode mules down from Meqdela to Islamgee and the royal camp. Having been imprisoned for so many months, they were astonished at the spaciousness of the amba and the plateau below. They found Theodore seated on a pile of stones overlooking the bottom of the road where thousands of his men were preparing to drag the army's artillery pieces up the steep ascent. The King was relaxed, and intent on the activity below. There was a curve in the road that seemed to preclude a successful outcome, and he motioned the Englishmen to come and sit behind him. He would never have trusted an Abyssinian in such a position – one slight push would have sent him toppling over a precipice. In a few minutes he began to chat pleasantly, noticing that both he and Rassam had aged in the last few months, but that his hair was by far the grayer. Catching his light mood, Rassam joked back that as the King was a married man, his cares were far greater. Theodore was delighted with the repartee and sent Ayto Samuel, who was translating, to call Waldmeier to enjoy the joke. He then walked down to the curve in the road to direct the difficult maneuver required to turn "Sebastopol". The noise of the thousands laboring was immense, but the King had only to lift his hand, and there was absolute silence. Then his clear voice rang out in total control. The big gun, probably weighing close to seven tons, was turned safely and the King leaned back to regale the Englishmen with the story of his trip. He then sent them back to their tent on the amba where he had asked Susan

Waldmeier and Mary Saalmuller to prepare a meal. (3, pp. 376-9) This was the last time they were to see him as he could be at his best – cheerful, confident and charming.

~

By the 9th of April the leading British forces were visible through the King's telescope. The day before, Theodore had ordered all of the native Abyssinian prisoners on Meqdela to come down to Islamgee, and he had released most of the women and children – close to two hundred in number. On this morning, watching the British come down the same road that he, the King, had labored to build, his mood grew darker and darker. This engineering marvel, his great source of pride, would facilitate his own destruction. He was struggling to move his cannons to Fahla, where they would overlook the advance of the British across the Bashilo, when a tremendous storm broke over Islamgee. As it subsided the King heard some of the remaining Abyssinian prisoners crying out for food. In an insane burst of anger he called to his Chiefs and, himself, went to begin a hideous butchery. Many of these prisoners were there on the most trivial charges. They were called out one by one and thrown over a precipice. Those who survived the fall were shot, and all left for the vultures and hyenas. One poor victim had his two sons with him. The boys were thrown over the edge and their father was set free. (6, p. 316) Waldmeier and Saalmuller were horrified witnesses of the atrocities, fearing that at any moment they, too, would be noticed and hurled to oblivion. Rassam had been warned to stay out of sight in his tent. Only nightfall brought an end to the fearful rampage.

Early the next morning (Good Friday, the 10th of April) Waldmeier and Karl Saalmuller were called to the King's tent. Upon their arrival they found Theodore in a foul mood, but apparently he had changed his mind about their summons. They were left to stand about in anticipation of the next jolting turn of events. When Theodore reappeared he sent orders that the English Mission should at once go back up to the fortress at Meqdela, which seemed a very threatening sign to the remaining Europeans. Almost simultaneously, a letter arrived from Sir Robert Napier to the King formally announcing his arrival and demanding the surrender of all European prisoners. The King refused to notice the letter and, turning to Waldmeier, told him to go and bid farewell to his wife and child as he was soon to die by the side of a King. (7, p. 108) All of the troops at both Meqdela and Islamgee, with a very few left to guard Meqdela, were assembled and marched off to Fahla. Here the King harangued them with accounts of past exploits, and they rushed down upon the forefront of the British army. In the excitement of the advance, one of the large cannons near which Theodore was standing was double charged and exploded. The rest of the artillery shot down on the English troops, who returned fire on the rushing Abyssinians with breech loading rifles. There was a dreadful slaughter in their front lines, and the remainder of Theodore's army turned back to Fahla. The King was in a fury, and the European artisans and prisoners who had witnessed the battle were warned that they would be executed, but during the night the King called for Waldmeier and Mr. Flad and sent them to Rassam, up on Meqdela, to ask for his advice. (7, p. 111)

The faithful Ayto Samuel awoke Rassam in the early morning hours. The English mission had gone to bed ignorant of the decisive British success over Theodore's fighters. Neither side had had any appreciable success with their artillery. It was the English rifles, capable of firing six shots a minute, which had decided the battle. The message from the King was that while he had expected the British to fight like women, he had been wrong. Now he needed his friend's help. Rassam had always counseled the King to seek peace with the British. It was agreed that Theodore should send Lieutenant Prideaux, Mr. Flad and his own son-in-law, Dejazmach Alamy, to negotiate with Robert Napier. These three men crossed the British lines early on the morning of April 11th. (6, p. 319)

The King waited anxiously for a response for most of that day. Finally, at about three o'clock in the afternoon, a brief letter from Napier arrived. It was firm and to the point. The King must submit to the Queen of England and all of the Europeans in his hands should be delivered to the British camp that day. If these conditions were met, he and his family would be treated honorably.

Theodore was enraged. What did honorable treatment mean? Would the British help him to fight his enemies or would he be held as a prisoner? He had already begun to draft a second letter – long and rambling – to Napier, and giving Lieutenant Prideaux and Mr. Flad very little time to catch their breath, sent them back to the British camp. This time Sir Robert did not even take time to write a response, but sent Prideaux and Flad back to reiterate his first message orally. It was while waiting for their second return that Theodore called together his principal chiefs and the European artisans to discuss options, but soon became so over excited that they had difficulty in restraining him from suicide. The royal anger was now at a fearful pitch, and the chiefs were criticizing his weakness and advising a blood-thirsty demise for all of the Europeans. Some recommended burning them alive and others to cut off their hands and feet and leave them for the British to discover. (7, p. 113) But in a while Theodore's anger began to wane and, dismissing the chiefs, he sent Karl Saalmuller and a Mr. Meyer (another one of the European artisans) to ready themselves to escort the British mission and the other European prisoners to the English camp. Two chiefs and Ayto Samuel were sent to alert this group to move as quickly as possible. The chiefs and Samuel were utterly despondent. Everyone, the Europeans included, expected that the Mission would be murdered on their way out of Theodore's stronghold.

Ayto Samuel was convinced that their only hope was to delay their exodus so that Theodore's anger might have time to subside. Against Rassam's explicit instructions he suggested to the King that he should take time to bid farewell to this good friend.

And so they proceeded on the path down the side of amba Meqdela. Rassam and Dr. Blanc had once again donned their dark blue government uniforms. They were followed by Consul Cameron, Dr. Stern, Mr. and Mrs. Rosenthal, and Mr. Kerans. Rassam had been warned by Waldmeier to try to keep Dr. Stern as inconspicuous as possible. On across Islamgee they rode their mules when, suddenly, Rassam was pulled aside. At Ayto Samuel's prompting Theodore had decided to see his friend one last time. He was standing at the cross in the road of the upper and lower paths leading down from Islamgee and Fahla, and came to sit with Rassam. There he ruminated on their chances of meeting again either in this world or the next, and then quietly motioned him to leave. (6, pp. 322-4)

Dr. Blanc and the others had been stopped while Rassam and the King talked. When they were motioned to continue forward, Dr. Blanc looked up and saw Theodore, with twenty hand-picked riflemen behind him, standing on some rocks above. The King had just turned to one of his men to reach for his gun. All seven of the Europeans were sure that their final moment had come, but when the King turned back, his eyes rested on the doctor. For just a moment he seemed to hesitate, and then, slowly, he lifted his hand in farewell. Karl Saalmuller and Mr. Meyer hastened to escort the prisoners on down to the English camp.

The next morning was Easter Sunday. Sir Robert Napier sent Karl and Mr. Meyer back to Theodore to urge him to release the remaining European missionaries and artisans with their families to the British camp. The King had just sent a conciliatory letter to Napier along with a peace offering, in the manner of Abyssinia, of hundreds of cows and sheep. In the confusion of information passing back and forth, Theodore understood that the gesture had been agreeable to the British. While this was not true, Theodore's understanding may have provided the impetus for him to let the remaining Europeans go. With what joy did Theophilus Waldmeier and Karl Saalmuller go to Susan and Mary, and urge them to hasten their preparations for departure. In kindness, the two men also took leave of the King. By late afternoon fifty-nine Europeans, including children, entered the British camp. After so many years (for Theophilus and Karl it had been ten) they walked as in a dream. For all – the English Mission, the original prisoners, the missionaries and the artisans – it took a long while to put the dreadful excesses and the fear of imminent death behind them.

Looking down on the British camp, Theodore began to perceive that he have been duped. Robert Napier had no real understanding of the meaning of the gift of cows and sheep that to an Abyssinian meant reconciliation. As evening gathered, from his heights Theodore could see that none of the animals had been taken into the British camp. Suspecting deception, he was convinced that he would be captured and either held in chains or executed. His own soldiers were slipping away, but a few last loyal friends refused to leave. They returned to the top of the amba with the King and the next morning, with him, fought to the death as the British stormed Meqdela. The faithful Prime Minister, Ras Ingida, died at his side; and at the very last, Theodore shot himself rather than to submit to capture. (6, p. 324) In the end, these few old soldiers died with valor.

~

The next day Theodore was buried at the little church on the heights of Meqdela, and the British army began its return to the coast. Arriving at Zulla on the Red Sea, most of the European survivors of Meqdela embarked on the steamer, *Ottawa*, destined for Suez. From there the little family group of Waldmeiers and Saalmullers took a train to Cairo, and then on to Alexandria to travel by ship to the area of Palestine. Theophilus, Susan and little Rosa went inland to Jerusalem and eventually north to the Lebanon. Karl and Mary remained on the coast at Jaffa (Tel-Aviv) and worked in a mission station there. It was here that their lives began to take on a more normal course, and here that they began to raise their family of daughters.

It is significant to my family's story that Theophilus traveled to the Lebanon. There, for the first time, he encountered Quaker missionaries, and he was quickly drawn to their simple faith. In the little village of Brummana, on the slopes of Mt. Lebanon, he was able to gather their support to build a mission house and a training school for boys. During the summer of 1874 Theophilus traveled to England in connection with this work and, upon his return, was greeted with streams of tears. The family had all been ill, and Mary's daughter, little Dora Saalmuller, who had been visiting from Jaffa for the summer, had died. Nevertheless, in October of that year Theophilus was able to purchase a plot of land at Brummana that came to be known as Ain Salaam, or the fountain of peace. The mission house was soon under construction, and Theophilus was able to persuade Karl and Mary to come and join him and his family on the burgeoning campus. The experiences of Abyssinia were consigned to the past. There was a future to look forward to, and a new home.

In Their Generations

Mary Bell Saalmuller

BIBLIOGRAPHY (PART II)

1. Armbruster, Stephana. Life and History of John Bell and his Descendants. Palma de Mallorca: 1966.
2. Baker, Samuel W. Exploration of the Nile Tributaries of Abyssinia. O. D. Case & Co. Hartford: Francis Dewing & Co. San Francisco: 1868.
3. Blanc, Henry. A Narrative of Captivity in Abyssinia. London: Frank Cass & Co. Ltd. 1970.
4. Marsden, Philip. The Barefoot Emperor. Harper Perennial: London: 2008.
5. Rassam, Hormudz. Narrative of the British Mission to Theodore, King of Abyssinia. Vol I, John Murray, London: 1869.
6. Rassam, Hormuzd. Narrative of the British Mission to Theodore, King of Abyssinia. Vol II, John Murray, London: 1869.
7. Waldmeier, Theophilus. Ten Years in Abyssinia. The Orphans Printing Press, Leominister.

In Their Generations

PART III

FOUR SISTERS

*And on that cheek and o'er that brow
So soft, so calm, yet eloquent,
The smiles that win, the tints that glow,
But tell of days in goodness spent, –
A mind at peace with all below,
A heart whose love is innocent.*
     —Lord Byron

ETHIOPIA
EARLY 20th CENTURY

- ERITREA
- RED SEA
- Asmera
- Adwa
- Aksum
- Gondar
- Lake Tsana
- Debra Tabor
- SIMIEN MTS
- Bure
- Debra Markos
- Blue Nile
- Djibouti
- Dire Dawa
- ADDIS ABABA
- ETHIOPIA

In Their Generations

Four Sisters

Wega Miller George

Little Dora was gone, but there were four other children to come along in the Saalmuller home, all of them girls. My mother always said that her grandfather chose the loveliest names he knew for his daughters. Beauty is, of course, in the mind of the listener, but perhaps he did well enough. The eldest was Sarona (Ona to the family); followed by Stephana, or Fana, (because she was born on St. Stephen's day); Wega (the 'W' is, of course, pronounced as a 'V') and Maria. She was the baby, and known to all as Marilie. All four grew to adulthood, although Auntie Ona died in childbirth when she was a young woman. The others lived well into their eighties and Stephana, past one hundred.

In the 1870's Theophilus Waldmeier was busily purchasing land and building a campus, sponsored by British and American Quakers. It would eventually include a mission house, a boy's training school (where he and his family lived), a girl's school, a School of Industry and a hospital. To this bustling community he enticed his brother-in-law to look after the property and the cultivation of the land, but especially to take charge of the School of Industry. Karl Saalmuller was also to act as an assistant architect and the head of the entire program when Theophilus was off in Europe raising money. Theophilus well knew Karl's practical capabilities. It is astonishing that while he recognized his loyalty and his usefulness, he never mentioned Karl's name in his autobiography once the two of them had left Abyssinia. The Saalmuller family did not seem to feel slighted by Theophilus' predominance, and always spoke of him with great affection.

So the girls grew up in the lovely mountains above Beirut in the little town of Brummana. Their Lebanese neighbors were Maronites, Druzes, Christians and Moslems, including Sunni and Shia. The children spoke German, French, Arabic, English and snatches of their mother's native Amharic. From Beirut to Brummana was a three-hour ascent on horseback. The trek was described in 1887 by an English visitor:

"A drive of about 15 minutes first brought us outside the town [of Beirut] among the fields of mulberry trees and prickly pear.... The road began at once to ascend and grew narrower and rockier as we got higher. We passed through a mountain gorge and then up a steep stony pathway which the horses climbed nimbly and without the least hesitation, though my saddle must have been at an angle of 75 [degrees] the greater part of the way....[T]he path grew steeper, till it became a regular staircase!" (3, pp 39-40)

Their parents had early recognized the need for a place to house the many visitors who came from abroad, and built a family hotel nestling in the pine trees with a magnificent view of the Mediterranean Sea far below. This is where the Saalmullers lived and, while their father worked at the Quaker mission nearby, their mother took charge of the day to day care of the hotel and its guests. Built of native stone with a red tile roof, the family still owned and operated this lovely haven one hundred years later. (My brother and I were taken there to visit early in 1939 when we were quite young, but were hurried back home across the Atlantic that summer with the fear of U-boats palpable in the air.) I have two cherished pen and ink drawings of the building – one, a view of the terrace looking out through shrubbery and trees to the distant Mediterranean below; and the other, a view from the path beneath up to the solid, three-storey structure with its patios and porches surrounded by pines and a lone, statuesque cypress.

~

In the late 1880's the girls were marrying and leaving home. Sarona was the first to go, but sadly, did not survive her first pregnancy. Stephana was next, but made an unhappy choice and remarkably, for that day, divorced. The youngest, Maria, met a Frenchman of Huguenot descent whose parents had come to the Lebanon when he was just four years old. Adrien Bonfils spoke Arabic like a native and was a professional photographer when he met Marilie. They were married from the family's hotel and eventually made their home in Paris. I met her there once, when I was on holiday from college in England and she was comfortably retired in her son-in-law's hotel on the Rue Montmartre.

~

Stephana's second marriage was a delight. They called each other Ratty and Mole, after the two whimsical animal characters in Kenneth Grahame's *The Wind in the Willows*. Charles Armbruster was in the British consular service and had traveled extensively in Africa and the Near East. In this respect he was reminiscent of Fana's grandfather, John Bell. A graduate of Kings' College, Cambridge, he had gone out to Africa to serve first in the British Central Africa Protectorate Administration and then in the Sudan Political Service. It was during these years that his ability as a linguist emerged. The policy of the Service was not to allow its officers to sit isolated in an office but to have them continuously traveling about in the countryside. Armbruster became fluent in Arabic, and then commenced a serious study of first Nubian and then Amharic. Because of his understanding of the language of Ethiopia, he was sent on a series of missions to that country between 1906 and 1912. It was in 1912, when on leave in the Lebanon, that he met and married Stephana Saalmuller. Almost immediately after they returned to Sudan, he was appointed British Consul for the northwestern section of Ethiopia, and sent out to tour his new jurisdiction. The newlyweds departed Khartoum by train for Port Sudan on the 7th of December, 1912. Fana recorded the events of the trip to her mother's homeland with a newly acquired, anglicized witticism, but also with a concern for the land and an appreciation of its loveliness.

On the 12th of December Charles and Fana repacked their boxes and boarded the cargo ship, *Almeria,* bound for Djibouti. Arriving three days later, their ship lay two miles off shore and they, with their baggage, were taken in on a patrol launch, arriving at their hotel at about noon. Evidently, Fana found it all quite dirty and untidy. The room where she and Charles took their meals was furnished with a sewing machine, a broken mirror and numerous Japanese pictures hanging askew. They called on the Abyssinian Consul, Ayto Joseph, who returned their call the following day.

From Djibouti they headed inland toward the new Ethiopian capital, Addis Ababa. The first leg of their journey was accomplished by train as far as Dire Dawa – an eleven hour trip and, in those days, the end of the rail line.

As soon as the train stopped all sorts of people crowded in. One of the stoutest women we had ever seen, bagged us for her hotel. This was Mme. Fariorr (whom Fana refers to subsequently as "old mother beer barrel"). *Meanwhile two Abyssinian chiefs had introduced themselves to Charles and were making all sorts of polite inquiries. We put Hailye [our] Abyssinian Secretary in charge of the baggage, as we were afraid that the escort that had come to meet us might help themselves to some of it. Aito Demissyeh and Aito Darmaka and fourteen soldiers carrying rifles accompanied us up the street to the hotel. (Fana's diary)*

    Charles and Fana were relieved to arrive at their hotel and rid themselves of their escort, only to be thrust into the embrace of old mother beer barrel. Their room was crowded with furniture with one little bed in the center. When Charles asked for another to be put up for him he received an impassioned lecture on appropriate sleeping arrangements for married couples. Charles and Fana were touched by Mme. Fariorr's sense of conjugal propriety, and pitied her husband. But the food was good, they had their own private dining room and Charles and Fana began to organize supplies for their trek inland. By the 18th they had pitched tents outside of the town and their men and the muleteers were housed in them, and by the next day they had moved in as well and were putting their caravan together. At night, to Fana's great discomfort, hyenas howled near their tent. They spent the next few days visiting dignitaries, writing letters and shopping for supplies for the next six months. Charles wrote up his government accounts and worked hard on a proof of the multi-volume Amharic dictionary he was crafting. They hoped to leave on the 24th, but it was Christmas afternoon before they climbed onto their mules and headed for the interior. That first night they camped in a dry water course, sat by a fire, decried all towns and centers of civilization and watched the moon rise.

    They were up early to a beautifully fresh morning in sight of gazelle, dikdik, wild pigeons and partridges. Their trail led upward, climbing steep and rough mountain paths, and the air grew colder. Fana likened the atmosphere to a heavy, Scots mist. Charles suddenly turned in his saddle and wished her a happy birthday. They had both nearly forgotten.

    During the last days of the year they were generally trekking at a height of 7,000 feet, and passed through lovely woods of juniper and cedar. Some of the trees were 150 feet tall with a diameter at the base of 5 feet. Fana noticed areas of trees that had died by having their bark stripped off, and mourned their ruthless destruction by local farmers. The year ended with a fine, sunny day. Charles did accounts and paid the muleteers. After tea he and Fana went for a walk and collected plants for pressing. They came across a troop of about a dozen monkeys and on their way back to camp they spotted a lovely red and green parrot sitting on a branch eating berries, "… a very fine bird."

Fana and Charles began the new year at a slightly lower, and warmer, altitude. For the first time since leaving Dire Dawa there was a decent source of water nearby. The Burka was clear and bubbling, and they stayed to wash everything and to repack their boxes. Addis Ababa was still three weeks away. Climbing for the next few days it became so cold that even with their hot water bottles they were chilled. They entered a district that was half Galla, half Amharic, and Fana passed a scathing judgment on the latter's Christianity which, she said, "… consists in a very dirty blue cord they wear around their neck." A splendid view of mountains was spoiled by a raging forest fire set to clear land for cultivation. It was heartbreaking to see the destruction of the magnificent forest.

By mid-January they came to a customs station at Hawash, and were able to telephone ahead to Addis Ababa for two riding mules to be sent out to them. On the 13th, after a steep descent, they came upon a large herd of camels with their backs covered by birds picking off flies. Just as Fana was beginning to feel very nervous about the noted, local Hawash lions, Charles cried out, "Look at the line!" He was exclaiming at the earth works of a new railway being built from the coast while she thought that he had seen a tawny attacker. They both dissolved in laughter.

Charles and Fana reached Addis Ababa on the 22nd of January and spent nearly a month there in the pleasant social rigmarole of diplomatic circles. They bought two small horses and christened them Tweedle Dum and Tweedle Dee, and by the 18th of February they were traveling again.

It took almost two weeks to arrive at the Blue Nile, and three days to climb to the bottom of the 5,000 foot gorge and back up again. Having reached the edge of the plateau and started down to the river, they very soon had to dismount and walk, holding on with both hands and feet. At about two-thirds of the way down, they were able to stop near a spring and camp for the night. The view was magnificent, with the river visible for miles in either direction. The next morning again they had to walk as best they could with the descent becoming increasingly steep. The mules were unloaded and the boxes were carried by the muleteers. Close to the bottom there were some very dangerous ledges and Charles nearly fell, looking in one direction while walking in another. Fana grabbed him just in time. At their crossing, the river was a hundred yards wide and three feet deep, with their ford slanting to 150 yards. Off they went on their little horses with the muleteers firing rifles to frighten off the crocodiles. After lunch on the opposite bank they saddled up again to begin the ascent, but soon had to dismount because the path was so very steep. Again they camped overnight within the gorge, and rested there the next day as both men and beasts were exhausted. They continued early the next morning with what Fana described as a really terrible climb for two hours, with the sun on their backs, until they reached the plateau of the Gojjam plain.

During the next few days they rode through the undulating plain of Gojjam, stopping to rest off and on when Charles would work on his dictionary. They crossed several thickly-wooded hills and valleys, and then they would be back on the grassy plain. The weather was hot, and the grass so dry that Charles was afraid of a prairie fire. One day two enormous jackals sitting down in broad daylight watched them as they passed. By the 11th of March they rode into Debra Markos where they expected to meet with Ras Hailu, the local chief. He was away, but his cousin sent food and drink and Charles called upon his deputy.

Charles and Fana visited the Church of Debra Markos (hill of St. Mark) and admired paintings done on cloth in a seeming Byzantine style. On the 14th there were more gifts from local dignitaries and a visit from an earlier friend, Gabriel Buctor, and his sister-in-law; but after dinner Fana became very unwell and Charles reported that she had a very bad night. What neither of them ever intimated in the diary was that Fana had miscarried what proved to be her only pregnancy - twins. She was so ill that Charles sent for a doctor from the British Legation in Addis Ababa. Gabriel's sister-in-law came to sit with her, the local dignitaries sent food and kind inquiries, and one of them brought a charm against the evil eye to wear on her left arm. On the 21st there was a grass fire near their campsite and Fana had to be carried, on her bed, a half mile to safety. Dr. Wakeman finally arrived on the 3rd of April, and Fana got up for the first time three days later.

They were back on the trail by the 14th, still seeking a meeting with Ras Hailu. At each village they approached, the local chief would turn out with his men and provide them with an escort of honor through his territory. By the 23rd they were only a few miles from the Ras' campsite, and now at every little village they passed through, their escort would increase until soon there were over 800 men plus a band of cavalry looking handsome in native costume. Still accumulating attendants, their escort numbered over 3,000 when they finally gained the campground the Ras had chosen for them. How reminiscent it was of Hormuzd Rassam's first visit to King Theodore, in much the same part of the country. Charles and Dr. Wakeman walked out to meet Ras Hailu, who dismounted his mule and walked back to their tents with them, holding Charles' hand all the while. He sat chatting with Charles, Fana and Wakeman for more than an hour, drinking coffee and eating chocolate and biscuits.

The next day the three visitors had a two hour lunch with

Ras Hailu that commenced with an elaborate washing of hands. They drank tej (honey wine) and were served a dozen different dishes, all containing varying amounts of cayenne. With each new dish the Ras would scoop some up on a bit of injera (a flat bread) and put it in the mouth of one of his guests. He prepared a morsel for Charles, and Fana, knowing her husband's aversion to highly seasoned foods, told the Ras that Charles was unable to eat spices, but that she enjoyed seasoning and would eat it for him. Ras Hailu laughed, and passed it on to her.

They spent three pleasant weeks with Ras Hailu. A handsome, powerfully built man with charming manners, he seemed to be well-respected among his people. He would send gifts of sheep, fresh butter, native bread, meat wat (a stew dish) and tej. In return, Fana would go to her kitchen tent, bake him cakes and send the chocolate and biscuits that he so enjoyed. He and Charles had long, agreeable chats and the visit was deemed a great success. By the 1st of May, Charles and Fana were again packing their boxes in preparation for the next leg of their journey.

Shaking hands with the Ras at his gate, where he slipped an ivory handled riding switch into Charles' hands and matching gold bangles into Fana's, they began a brief detour from their next diplomatic destination and veered to the west. They rode through beautifully wooded country and splashed across numerous streams. Crossing a spur of Mount Wombeta their guide pointed out a spring in a marshy meadow that he identified as the source of the Blue Nile. (Sixty years before, her grandfather had delighted in standing at this very spot.) There were a Kosso tree and a few bushes growing to the side of the spring. It was difficult to approach because of the black muck everywhere and little pools of water. Then a small stream trickled insignificantly down a lower side of Wombeta, and the great river was born. Turning back to the east, they trekked for ten miles until a hail storm forced them to camp, where they were surrounded by high mountain peaks through which shocks of thunder rumbled and echoed. It was very cold.

Now they pushed diligently toward Debra Tabor and a scheduled visit to Ras Wolda Giyorgis. The next milestone was the Portuguese bridge crossing back over the Blue Nile after it had exited Lake Tsana. Fana described the gorge here as 50 feet deep and up to 20 feet wide, cut by the river through black, volcanic rock. A mile further along they rode through a mass of gardenia bushes in bloom and scores of striped lilies. Charles stated flatly that they were brown and white, only conceding the next day that perhaps Fana was, after all, correct and that the stripes were magenta.

The days spent approaching Debra Tabor were cold and rainy. Charles sent word ahead to the Ras that they were approaching, and Wolda Giyorgis responded with gifts of food and livestock. Their meeting was arranged for the 21st of May, and at 9:00 in the morning Charles donned his government uniform and was escorted by one hundred of the Ras' troops to the Gibbi (palace) where there were five hundred more men to witness the official discourse. Charles stayed for about half an hour, and returned to his tents with the same escort. He noted that there had been no refreshments.

Turning westward, they reached the shores of Lake Tsana by the 25th. On route they took an afternoon off to hunt guinea fowl; Fana had no luck, but Charles bagged two. For the next few days they were happy to follow along the eastern shore of the great lake that reminded them so much of the Mediterranean Sea. The breeze off the water was fresh and they saw an enormous variety of waterfowl, but no hippos. There had been some along this way when Charles had visited five years before. By the end of the month they reached Gondar, where two months' mail was waiting for them. There were no official duties to be performed, but Charles had to spend long hours haggling with the muleteers to settle on terms for their trip to Asmara. Here they met an

Italian doctor who very kindly treated some of their porters and also the two ponies who were suffering from sores on their backs. The doctor took Fana to visit the ruins of the 17th century Fasiladas castle that she found well-preserved, imposing and picturesque. On the 31st of May, to Fana's delight, she and Charles were visited by an elderly gentleman, Alaka Gabru Desta, who remembered Plowden and Bell and who had been present at the wedding of Fana's parents in Gaffat.

Charles and Fana headed north from Gondar on the 3rd of June. They had to leave one of their porters behind in the care of Dr. Calo, along with Tweedle Dum. They journeyed through the Simien Mountains and were relieved to reach the Takeze River before the heavy rains had set in. The water in the riverbed was low and they forded with ease. On the 25th of June they camped about a mile outside of Aksum. In this ancient capital, where the Hebrew Ark of the Covenant is reputed to have found a home, Fana seemed to find even the tallest obelisks uninteresting. By now the weather was so hot that they often traveled at night by candlelight. They rode on to Adwa and on the 4th of July approached the Mareb River that was by then running hard with thick, brown water stirred up by recent rains. Fana was afraid to cross, so to boost her confidence Charles had her follow immediately behind one of the naggadyes. The man's mule soon floundered and he had to leap off its back and pull the animal back to shore. Their next attempt was successful.

The journey was nearly at an end. They reached Asmara by the 11th of July and the next day was Charles' birthday. Fana's understated notation in her diary reads, "…39 [and] a fine boy for his age". Charles spent the next few days writing up his reports, while Fana mended clothes and repacked boxes. They were both warmly entertained by the Italian diplomatic corps there at the coast. Charles was to go back to Khartoum to deliver his official report and return the tents and other heavy baggage, while Fana was to travel home to Brummana to visit her mother and the rest of the family. They would meet at Port Said at the end of the summer to go on to England for their long leave.

The following year is difficult to unravel, but from one veiled remark Fana included in her brief history of the family, it seems that she and Charles returned to a post at Gondar in Ethiopia until the onset of the First World War. Charles spent most of his free time in scholarly research to produce his Amharic-English dictionary. By 1915, with war raging in Europe, he was commissioned and posted to the Intelligence Corps and joined the Egyptian Expeditionary Force until 1919. During this period Fana went back home to Brummana. In 1919 Charles returned to the Sudan Political Service where he and Fana lived at Sinkat, near the coast of the Red Sea, until their retirement in 1926. Aside from the years of the Spanish Civil War, Charles and Stephana Armbruster spent the next thirty years in what she described as one of the loveliest situations in Europe. She and Charles built a rambling stone house on the western tip of the island of Majorca overlooking the Mediterranean Sea. Here Charles mapped out a garden and returned to his first love in his linguistic studies, Nubian, while Fana ran the household and entertained a continuous round of visitors. It was to this haven that her sister, Wega, came from Brummana in the mid 50's.

Stephana and Charles Armbruster

~

Wega Saalmuller, my grandmother, was the sister who stayed in the Lebanon. While the other girls married and left, Wega stayed and helped her parents to run the family hotel. But, of course, we must go back a few years. In 1887, when the man who was later to become her husband, Thomas Little, first came to Brummana, Wega was only ten years old. There are a few things that we can be sure of about her even then. She was very pretty, with dark eyes and a rather round face, she was multi-lingual and she loved to play the piano. I still have a red, hard backed book of Beethoven's sonatas in which she had inscribed her name. And over the ensuing years there was one thing that was very certain - she only ever loved one man, and that was Thomas Little.

He was a convinced Quaker, the product of Friends schools in the north of England. When Thomas Little was ten he was sent to the Friends school at Ackworth. The one comment we have about him during his three year stay there is that he had, "…a kindly disposition in helping weaker boys". (2, p.7) The remark was a telling one: Thomas Little spent the rest of his life caring for and teaching boys. He was actually teaching at a day school by the time he was thirteen and went on the next year as a junior teacher, to Penketh. Continuing in these sorts of apprenticeship positions he came, at the age of twenty, to the Friends school, Rawdon, near Leeds. His next ten years, spent there, were extremely happy ones, and the ideas and skills he learned at Rawdon became the foundation of his later philosophy of education.

It was at Rawdon that Thomas came to realize a very personal and consecrated faith, and it was there, at the meeting house, where he first spoke publicly under the influence of the Holy Spirit. In 1886, while on a sabbatical of rest and study in Munich, he began to think of foreign mission work. He had heard of the Friends Mission Station at Brummana in the Lebanon, applied to serve there and was accepted as the assistant master at the Boys' Training School to work under Lotfallah Rizkallah. My mother's sister-in-law, Ruth Little, copied extracts from his diary describing those early years at the school beginning in 1888. Reading these cullings of his thoughts, we become privy to his delight in introducing sports into the boys' curriculum and his innovative inclusion of experiments to augment their textbook exposure to science. And gradually, too, we trace his growing love for Wega Saalmuller.

January 6, 1888: We took the football out for the first time, as it was rather colder than it has been. What excitement! Each boy, as he got the ball must examine it, feel its weight, and turn it over. Such shouting and fun! After dinner we divided into sides and I tried to teach them to play to get goals, but with no rules except not to touch the ball with their hands.

January 7, 1888: Got some goal posts put up and made some attempt at placing the players. We had a more successful game. In the evening what a lot of complaints! Kicked shins, bruised knees, ankles and wrists, torn stockings, etc. Lotfallah Rizkallah said he thought it too dangerous a game if they got hurt so much. I feel inclined to put the ball away. We shall, however, wait until tomorrow and see what they think about it then.

January 8, 1888: Thermometer at 37 degrees. Thick hail. When we came out of meeting it was snowing.

January 9, 1888: Ground frozen over for the first time. Ice 3/8" thick on the playground. Theophilus Waldmeier and I began to slide and the boys, seeing us go so smoothly along, tried to do the same but soon came to ground! Those confident in their strength tried the same, with similar results, until, by experience, big and little began to treat the ice with respect. Snow balling.

Toward the end of January Thomas and the boys were attempting to level an area for a rough tennis court. When it seemed to be reasonably well prepared, he sent one of the little boys to bring Dr. Bishara Manasseh, Rosa Waldmeier's husband, to help him to demonstrate the game. Thomas' Arabic was still rough so the message delivered was that he was ill, and the doctor came running. "However, after a good laugh, we soon got down to play. The first ball the doctor hit went soaring up to the roof [of the boys' school] where it stuck, and it took him a long time to learn to hit properly." The incident was typical of Thomas Little's struggle to learn Arabic in his early years in the near East. There were no formal lessons for new arrivals, and Thomas often learned the language from the boys on the playground. For him, the playground was simply an open air classroom. Perhaps it was such early struggles that brought him so close to the boys. He spoke of them as "my boys" and, indeed, he completely gave himself to them. In turn, he became their beloved "Mualim Tuma", or Teacher Thomas.

The struggle to establish sports as a part of the program at the Training School continued. To that end, the boys themselves raised a modest amount of money by providing small services in the local community, and during Easter break they worked with Thomas on the playing ground digging, removing stones and even building an enclosing wall to define the football field. It served the school for many years. In the meantime the hazards of play continued.

March 2, 1888: Rested my leg today. It was kicked by Rashid on the 6th Day [Friday] at football.

March 14, 1888: My leg is not better yet. It seems very tedious, but I go every day and watch the boys play to guide them and see that they do not kick each other. One of the elder boys today asked me if the boys in England could play as well as they do now! Rassim, taking a kick, looks like a boy learning to dive. He takes a deep breath and then, with his mouth firmly closed, takes a short run, but his courage fails him and he has to go back and start again. Both sides, meanwhile, wait patiently until the ball shall be released from captivity by one noble effort.

Some cannot understand the mysteries of taking the "free kick" with a run, and must take it standing. Accordingly, they place themselves almost vertically over the ball and then commence to swing their leg like a pendulum, but with a series of spasmodic jerks, hardly able to make up their mind to send the ball at all. At last, the decision having been made, they find their foot imbedded in the sand. A cloud of sand arises out of which the ball is seen emerging in any direction but the right one.

Thomas Little's next scheme in the realm of sports was the construction of a swimming pool. Reaction to this proposal was distinctly divided, with Lotfallah Rizkallah bitterly opposed to the idea, sneering and laughing at the very thought. The Lebanese on the school's staff seemed to have a fastidious objection to bathing in the same water twice, and insisted that the boys would have no interest in learning to swim. Theophilus Waldmeier was encouraging and Susan was not, so the thought lay dormant for more than two years, but in the end the mission campus had its pool along with the football field and the tennis courts. Space for playing cricket was set aside soon after.

By the end of 1888 Thomas Little had been in Brummana for about a year and a half, and we read his first account of an encounter with Wega Saalmuller. She must have been just eleven years old.

December 12, 1888: I asked the 1st class to write their idea of a Friends meeting. Today they brought their answers. There were no good ones. One only mentioned private prayer. Wega Saalmuller brought a letter in which she attacked the Friends meetings because of their length. She said prayer should not be frequent; and she did not find that Christ held meetings, that he spoke against public prayer, and that silence is much better in the privacy of one's own room and alone....What a joy if I can have the pleasure of being the human messenger, leading her to Christ.

It would seem that she had caught his eye and that he would

have his work cut out for him. He gently recommended to her that she might like to spend perhaps half an hour each day seeking God privately to see if she did not receive a message of his love.

At the end of 1888 Thomas observed that there was never enough time for all that there was to do. There were too many books to read and too many letters to write. There were too many photographs to develop, there was Arabic to be learned and there were classes to teach. Above all he must carve out time to play with the boys, which was both pleasure and duty. But he did note that he had just conducted a very good Bible class on Christ's words 'that thou doest it quietly' and "…was surprised to hear Wega S. say afterwards that it was a very interesting class and not too long." Perhaps his kindly attention had won him her respect.

In February of the next year Thomas and the boys began work on a real lawn tennis court, carrying 40 cartloads of earth from the rocks at the south end of the football field to level the ground. The work was completed and the grass grown and mown by mid July, and there was an official opening by the Mission Center's committee on the 27th. With hard physical labor and perseverance, Thomas was creating a new Rawdon at Brummana.

There were other struggles – less physical, but wearing nonetheless. He had a serious argument with a member of the teaching staff about what he called the "kind" system of dealing with the boys. L. H. (this is the only way in which he refers to this person) was becoming disenchanted with a gentle approach to discipline and saying that the boys were more attentive and learned their lessons better when threatened with a stick. Thomas was "… much disappointed to hear him say so and exhorted him to patience. [L. H.] tells me they used to bastinado the boys and that the stick was always kept on the desk for the purpose of beating them". Thomas insisted on kindness.

Perhaps his greatest innovation at the Boys Training School was in his method of teaching science. If there had been any instruction of natural science before his arrival, it had been entirely from a book. Thomas introduced the use of experiments to inform the children, and would include the girls from their school in his classes, and any others from the neighborhood so interested. The exercises were basic and the apparatus simple. An example was the great interest he generated in the "mosquito bottle", an old pickle jar hung up in the school dining room in which many wondering children watched the development of the insect. Talk would be extended to include the topic of public health, and "Mualim Tuma" and his boys would be seen making their rounds to any pools of standing water in the neighborhood carrying their cans of paraffin to destroy mosquito larva.

After serving in Brummana for two years, the committee in England raised Thomas Little's allowance to 60 pounds per annum. He was not at all pleased to hear this news for he did not want his work to be a matter of money. He reconciled himself to the increase by rationalizing that he could return the money in various charitable ways. A year later he was beginning to feel the need to challenge himself further.

February 9, 1890: I became impressed today with the conviction that sometime in the future (probably when I know Arabic sufficiently) God will need me to begin pioneer work by myself and alone – unless indeed He sees fit to provide me with a wife....I have long felt that we are too comfortable here and do too little work for the people round about.

It would seem that even in moments of devout commitment to his work; Wega Saalmuller would steal, uncalled, into a corner of his heart. Two months later there is a rather puzzling entrance in his journal.

April 20, 1890: Had a talk with Wega Saalmuller today arising out of a simple question as to how she liked the meetings. She seemed more satisfied than she had been before and after a quarter of an hour or so, she was ready to go.

April 21, 1890: After the Scripture Union reading today we had a time of unbroken silence. No remarks and no vocal prayer, which was perhaps just as well. I had hoped for an opportunity to speak to W. S. today and am sorrowful that she has not been able to report any progress in the matter of which we spoke yesterday.

What that matter might have been we are not told. She was thirteen years old, intelligent and independent. She would find her own way.

In July he learned of his brother's pending marriage back home in England and wrote to his future sister-in-law, a letter redolent of his kindly nature and firm convictions.

My dear Jessie, I know little of conventionalities so I hope thou wilt excuse me if I am, through ignorance, breaking any in thus addressing thee. All I know is that my dear brother has taken thee to his heart and that therefore, it is not merely my duty, but my privilege, to look forward to that happy moment when before our Heavenly Father, thou wilt be numbered amongst our now scattered family.... No doubt thou hast become acquainted with the way in which the Lord led me to leave my father's house and to make my home in the Lebanon among these interesting...people. Missionary life has its lights and shadows; its joys and sorrows. The disappointments and sorrows are often bitter, but the joys of being about our Father's business, the joys of leading people to our own dear loving Saviour far, far outweigh all earthly troubles and spiritual discouragement; and the peace of mind and spirit is something very real, proceeding from the Heavenly Presence within....

By early in the next year Thomas Little's thoughts and attention turned more and more toward Wega Saalmuller. They were constantly thrown together in the intimate school community. She and her sisters were day students at the girls' school that, now with the innovation of co-education that

Thomas fostered, shared classes and activities with the boys. She was both challenge and fulfillment to the goodhearted English Quaker who spent his days serving the children and his God.

<u>March 13, 1891</u>: After supper Wega was alone playing the piano so I invited her to my [office] for a quiet talk on a matter which had been troubling me for some time. She was very reluctant to come, but after much hesitation she did so. At the conclusion of our talk we bowed together in silent prayer for some time and then she departed. I feel happy to think she had put herself in God's hands.

<u>April 25, 1891</u>: We are much troubled at the illness of Jos[eph] Fakhar who had a stroke of paralysis. The first week E. Clayton went to the nurses' Home and today Wega went. It has been very nice to see such a change in her lately. Today before she went I asked her not to forget to pray for us and she said so nicely and prettily, "Of course not."

<u>May 13, 1891</u>: This morning Wega joined me in prayer in my [office], chiefly concerning some trouble she was having upstairs which she found very hard to bear. In the afternoon we had a game of tennis and, after that, a long talk and, of course, thanksgiving. I went to bed very happy. Of course I feel the strange position in which I am placed by these talks with Wega, and the construction people may put upon them, but God knows all and I try to follow where He leads.

Thomas was having his effect. Wega was beginning to accept his fundamental premise that God should be central to all of life – thoughts, actions and relationships. It was not that Karl Saalmuller and his family were areligious – after all, Karl had gone as a lay missionary to the wilds of Abyssinia – but both his background in the church and Mary's were strongly liturgical. It was Theophilus Waldmeier who had made the dramatic change to join the Society of Friends: the Saalmullers had never done so. Now all four of their daughters were being educated in a school financed by the Friends' Foreign Mission Association.

Thomas Little's devotion to Wega was changing her perspective and, through her, her sisters were also influenced.

<u>May 30, 1891</u>: Sitt Wega has gone through many troubles lately and we have talked and prayed together. Yesterday I walked to the Hotel with Sarona, and on the way I felt impelled to ask her if she was saved, to which she replied, "No." I invited her…to talk the matter over. She agreed at the time, but later excused herself. However, I waited and prayed. Today Sitt Wega brought her to me and left us together. After much prayer and discussion she said that all had become plain to her and that she would put herself in God's hands. I warned her not to marry Mr. Meyer until he had gone through the same experience, and then she left. So our prayers are once again answered. Sitt Wega was also very pleased.

The 10th of June was Wega's fourteenth birthday. Thomas and some of the boys went to sing to her. She and Thomas had become very close, but were still not without disagreement.

<u>July 14, 1891</u>: Since then [her birthday] we have had many happy times together and many spiritual conflicts have taken place.

<u>July 31, 1891</u>: A week of much earnest praying about Sitt Wega. The thing that troubles my mind is that she may slide back in her young Christian faith, and become apathetic. She has so many troubles. I trust that my sadness does not arise from anything personal.

By October he realized that he was deeply in love, but had not yet sorted it all out in his mind.

<u>October 2, 1891</u>: I have been in Beirut for nearly two weeks – at the Glockler's and at the Tower's – to write my circular letter. My thoughts have been much turned to Sitt Wega, as to whether it is God's will that I should take any steps towards entering into a nearer relationship [with her]. I have asked Him to guide me as He has in all other things, as everything seems to be accumulating to throw us more together. I have put myself

unreservedly in His hands and do not wish, by some indiscretion, to disturb His plans.

December 19, 1891: Sitt Wega has often been ill in body and it seemed my duty to help her as much as possible. I have often prayed about it that I may be guided aright. Just now she is in bed upstairs with severe neuralgia brought on by weak health, a bad tooth, and a cold [caught] journeying up from Beirut after having been there to consult the dentist and have leeches applied. I have had very little spiritual work among the boys this year, so far. Sometimes I have thought that the Lord was leading me to give all my attention to Sitt Wega. It seems as if the boys are hardly ripe for any spiritual work, and as if more public work were needed. Perhaps the Lord seeks to teach me some lesson by all this.

Thomas Little was certainly in love, and it was all-consuming. Even his boys were to take second place for a short time. While he was not quite sure exactly how to proceed, there was no doubt in his mind about his feelings for Wega Saalmuller. My grandmother seems to have had her share of growing pains, both physical and mental, but she had, as well, acquired a devoted confidant.

January 9, 1892: This evening, as I walked toward Beit Meri after 8:30 with Mr. Glockler, I opened my mind to him regarding Wega, telling him the story from the beginning and asking him what he thought about it. He entered fully into sympathy with my perplexity and we discussed the matter together, which left me feeling much more settled in my mind than I had been before. I believe I love Wega more than anyone in the world and would do anything for her.

January 28, 1892: Yesterday Wega was in much trouble and distress, and also very angry. I spend a lot of time with her and my work is seriously interfered with; but I believe it is God's will that it should be so. He has some future for her, no doubt – whether to take her place at the head of the school or in some other sphere, I do not know.

<u>February 15, 1892</u>: I expect to go to England very soon now. My love for Wega has much increased and it will be very hard for us to part. If this feeling lasts during the coming months, I suppose it is true love and a sign from God.

He left Beirut for England on the 8th of March for a six month visit to include a joyous reunion with his family, consultation concerning his work with other Quakers at home, and a tour of Friends Schools in the British Isles. Chats with his family invariably included references to his relationship with Wega Saalmuller. She filled his thoughts, and his concern for their future relationship left him worried and, sometimes, depressed. She was so very young, untried in the ways of the world and new to the faith of the Friends. How could he be sure of the way forward? What was he to do?

<u>April 10, 1892</u>: At Wilmslow, to consult E. Pearson about Sitt Wega. Although I have seen things move already and have had all difficulties removed, and much encouragement, yet at the same time I have been weighed down by a great oppression which I cannot describe. It is always with reference to my thoughts of marriage. I cannot believe it [the oppression] comes from God and therefore conclude that it comes from the Evil One. It is terrible, taking away all buoyancy of spirit. I am constantly asking God to make things plain so that I may do His will.

<u>April 13, 1892</u>: Have been through a severe, proving time, in which I have been brought very low. I miss Wega very much yet at such times as these, when I am much oppressed, I wonder if I am doing the right thing in asking her to marry a poor missionary.

And then, suddenly, there is a sort of release and he is at peace with his decision. There have been kind friends to listen and his dear family to encourage and support him. The doubts have vanished, and Thomas is sure that he must proceed with his hope to marry Wega Saalmuller.

<u>April 14, 1892:</u> After having talked again with Edward, [his brother] and after spending all day in prayer, I at last placed the letter I had written in the G. P. O. [General Post Office] – with a prayer on my lips and in perfect peace of mind. Since then …my joy has been great and my love has increased. What the end is to be I do not know. All my friends at home assure me that we are as good as married.

Her answer reached him just over a month later when he was on his tour of schools and packing up to leave Ireland. The letter had been forwarded to him in his travels and was, by the time it was put in his hands, enclosed in three envelopes – a fit symbol of its importance. It was given to him as he was about to leave an empty schoolroom, where he found welcome quiet and solitude to read Wega's acceptance of his proposal. He felt as if his mind was leaping out to Brummana in love and joy. Thomas was still obligated to continue his tour, but would return to the Lebanon toward the end of October. In August, still on tour, he wrote of his deep contentment and happiness.

<u>August 14, 1892:</u> I have had a much easier time during the last week or two, getting more sleep at night and losing entirely the weariness in the head that I brought with me from Brummana. I don't get any more of those dreadful fits of depression. That I love her more than anyone else in the world there is no doubt, but I sometimes wonder whether she is fit to occupy her place at the head of the school, being so young. But this matter, like all else, is in God's hands. I find strength and happiness in the thought that with God's help, my darling Wega will soon learn and become not only all that could be desired, but much more – so I rest in God and go forward with confidence and hope.

Thomas was able to return to the Lebanon on the 22nd of October. His steamship anchored out in the Beirut harbor and, as the ship's boat from the steamer carried him in to the dock;

Wega, with her father and Stephana, motored out into the harbor to greet him. So, newly engaged, they saw each other for the first time in months and could only shout and wave at each other across the water. But, in the evening, when the excitement had worn off and he had managed to clear himself through customs; Thomas hired a carriage and he and Wega rode alone together up the hills to Brummana.

Now there was a quiet wedding to plan and furnishings for their home to be bought. They would live quite simply in the rooms of the Boys Training School that the Waldmeier's had originally occupied. Thomas feared that somehow they would live too elaborately. On the day before their wedding he wrote:

I am so afraid that we shall get too luxurious in our furniture. Miss Dobbie has given us divan covers of rich workmanship and I have bought a piano for Wega. These things will require suitable furniture to accompany them and our difficulty will be to keep as a missionary should be – in the simplicity of Christ. It is my prayer that we may be so enabled to do.

And so they were married. She was just fifteen and he was a full twenty years her senior. She tended to be ebullient and passionate. He was quiet and thoughtful; she was musical and a linguist, he was an educator and an innovator; she suffered various physical complaints, he was a robust sports enthusiast. They would have just sixteen years together, but they would be happy years, filled with the rough and tumble of school boys and their own little brood. She was barely thirty when he died, never considered remarrying and lived well into her eighties. On the morning of their wedding day, November 17, 1892, he wrote, "Have been to see that everything is right at the Meeting House. I have been packing up for our journey to Damascus.... We had a sweet time of prayer together this morning, Wega and I."

Thomas' trust in his wife's ability to grow in her new role in the Boys' Training School was well-placed. She welcomed and entertained visitors, mothered school boys, participated in special school programs and shared her music. The days bustled with cheerful activity. Keenly interested in co-education, Thomas initiated joint lectures for the staffs of both the boys' and the girls' schools and began shared classes for the pupils. Routine evening gatherings for the children's parents were begun, and so Thomas launched the embryo of a parent-teacher association. Wega would accompany her husband to these community gatherings to act as a hostess and to dramatize his vision of family participation.

The next year Thomas began to address the linguistic deficiencies of newly arriving Friends missionaries. No longer dependent for vocabulary from the boys on the playground, he now had a fluent Arabist by his side. He and Wega put together a series of lesson books with extensive, pertinent vocabularies to be available to newcomers and to visitors.

Early in 1895 Lotfallah Rizkallah died, quite suddenly, of cholera; and the entire responsibility for the Boys' Training School fell upon Thomas. As he had foreseen, Wega would be at his side as head of the school. She was now eighteen, and had already proven herself as an apt companion in his work. It was in this same year that he and Wega welcomed their first child, Sylvia, to be followed a year later by my mother, Vera. Thomas, with Quaker simplicity, would give only one name to each of his children, believing second, or middle, names to be excessive. The arrival of Charles (or Chas) in 1900 completed the family.

By 1902, Thomas Little had modified the curriculum of the Training School to meet the entrance requirements of the American University of Beirut, and at the same time the school was newly designated as the Boys' High School. The success of its early graduates making the transition to college, both in their demeanor and academics, underlined the rigor of their preparation and earned Thomas' school a reputation for excellence.

These were happy years for the young family. Thomas was recognized in the community for his work, and much loved by "his boys". Wega was known for her hospitality to visitors and care of the pupils. In later years my mother fondly remembered the fun of family camping trips her father would instigate. The mountains were beautiful with wildflowers in the spring, with her favorite, cyclamen, blooming in the shadow of the rocky hillsides. Their father taught the girls to play tennis, and Chas, soccer. The Saalmuller's hotel was a short walk from the school, so there were visits with their grandparents and whichever "Aunty" might be at home. Stephana was a particular favorite. Like their mother, the children grew up multi-lingual and loving music, and they became able students at their Father's school. It was an extraordinarily happy childhood.

In the school year of 1906-1907, the Friends Foreign Mission Association began to run a deficit and proposed to cut back on their funding of the Boys' High School. This was an enormous blow to Thomas Little, whose response was to try to raise more money from school fees by increasing the number of pupils. Physically, he had already suffered a near-drowning when rescuing one of the school boys, and had not seemed to recover his accustomed vigor. Now, his fear that the school would be crippled, put an enormous strain on an already weakened constitution. He canceled a long-scheduled sabbatical and threw himself into recruitment, extra teaching and additional administrative work. On the day before the school's Easter holiday in April of 1908, he suddenly collapsed and died. He was buried the next day, a man much loved and respected in Brummana and the surrounding villages. Stephana was home at the time and remembered that as his coffin was carried to the cemetery on the shoulders of the school boys' relatives, suddenly two men came forward and began to perform the historic sword dance of the Dreuse tribes – a tribute normally reserved to honor only their princes. (1, p. 31)

Wega Miller George

~

The Boys' High School had lost its chief advocate and Head Master; Wega and the three children had lost the center of their lives. I do not know what those first days were like. The loss was dreadful. They could not remain resident in the school, and retreated to the shelter of the Saalmuller family's hotel. As the years went by Wega, who had learned to welcome and entertain guests of the school, used these same skills in the family business. When her father died and her sisters had made their homes in Paris and in Majorca, it was she, with her mother and then she alone, who ran the hotel. She did not leave it until 1954 when she retired, at the age of seventy-seven, and went to live with Charles and Stephana Armbruster in their home at Puerto Andraitx on the island of Majorca.

But the children were another matter. Schooled as she was by Thomas on the merits of an education in the tradition of English Friends, Wega Little decided to take the children to England. She would support them with her earnings from the hotel, but she would place them in schools in Yorkshire near some of Thomas' brothers. My mother vividly recalled arriving in Darlington and being taken, with Sylvia and Chas, to visit some of their father's family. The three children had an uneasy fear that their mother was planning to put them up for adoption and conspired together to behave very badly so that no one would want them. Actually, they were placed in boarding schools and farmed out to visit various relatives and members of the Friends meeting during school holidays. Now separated from both parents, the shock was profound. All three received an excellent education, as their mother hoped. Sylvia was trained in nursing and my mother in primary education. Chas, who drew beautifully, became an artist and archeologist. Somehow, my mother, Vera, was able to throw herself unreservedly into both the academics and athletics of her new school, and embrace her new life. Years later she drew upon the memories of her early years and created, for my brother and for me, the sort of happy home that she had known as a child.

Returning to the Lebanon in the autumn of 1908, Wega Little committed herself to the work of running the family hotel. It had always been a comfortable building, enjoying a healthful setting and a magnificent view. Wega began to augment its reputation for hospitality with targeted attention for individual visitor's needs. The early years were kind, the business thrived and occasionally she was able to visit her children in England. My mother never questioned her devotion to them and tended to idolize her hard work and her lifelong loyalty to the memory of Thomas Little. Then suddenly, on June 28, 1914, Gavrilo Princip shot and killed the Archduke Franz Ferdinand of Austria, and everyone's life changed.

~

When World War I broke out, most Europeans in the Lebanon, even those working at the Friends schools in Brummana, quickly left for their homelands. Wega, knowing her children to be safe in England, stayed at the hotel with her mother where they were soon joined by Stephana. After all, the Lebanon was their home. The Boys' High School was assigned to the care of one of its early graduates, Tanius Cortas, who, with his wife, Mariam, and their children, moved into the School's family apartment to care for the mission property. As with so many families during these desperate years, Wega dug a hole in the kitchen garden, buried the family silver and then went to work. By the spring of 1915 the Turkish army had entered the area and occupied both the school and the hotel. When the army insisted that Tanius lead the school in saluting the Turkish flag every morning, he resigned. When food became scarce, Wega sought out Mariam Cortas to join her in assisting some of the local people. At first, the two women raised money to help feed nursing mothers. Then, with one Dr. Arthur Dray who was staying at Wega's hotel, they expanded their efforts to create a soup kitchen to provide one simple meal a day for the needy. Mariam Cortas offered her home from which to feed about fifteen persons. "... [W]ithin a week there were fifty to feed; a few days later 100. Mrs. Cortas could no longer feed this crowd from her door, and the kitchen was moved to a neighboring hotel [The Saalmuller's] which had been seized, occupied, and then abandoned by Turkish troops." (3, p. 159) By 1916, the Brummana soup kitchen (as it came to be called), working out of Wega's hotel, was daily feeding 1,500, and continued to provide relief both to local people and to Armenian refugees until the end of the war. (Throughout my childhood thirty years later and more, I was exhorted to remember the starving Armenians and never allowed to leave food on my plate.) The soup kitchen received contributions from some private funds held by American missionaries, and there were also contributions from wealthy citizens in Beirut. At the height of its operation it fed a maximum of 1,700 – mostly children and the rest, women. Strangely, officials in the Turkish government that was so determined to eliminate the local population, vied with each other to support the relief effort in Brummana. Wega emerged from the war as something of a local heroine. How very proud of her Thomas would have been.

After the war the three children returned home from England to begin their careers. What a joy it was to be back in the familiar mountains and to see, once again, the welcoming hotel; but all three soon gravitated to Cairo to find employment. Those early years were exciting. Sylvia worked as a nurse in an English hospital and rose quickly in her profession, Chas joined excavations of pyramids and Vera began teaching little children at an English school. The three enjoyed frequent visits with each other, and the trip home to their mother was an easy one.

In Their Generations

By the late 1920's both Vera and Chas were married, and Vera was a half a world away in the United States; but the hotel in Brummana thrived, Tanius Cortas had returned to reopen the Boys High School and the campus of schools and a hospital, first built by Theophilus Waldmeier, was busily engaged once more.

In 1939 it was all to do over again. Once more the Europeans associated with the mission campus were either on furlough or returned to their homelands and once more Wega Little buried the family silver in the kitchen garden and continued to work and to help her neighbors. Sylvia became a nurse to the British forces in Egypt and Chas with his wife and son went to Palestine and shared the American Friends' cottage in Ramallah with others of the Brummana mission. Vera, who had raced back to the United States after a visit there with my brother and me, could only write anxious letters and send packages. But by May of 1941 British forces had advanced back into the Lebanon and Wega was able to carry on at the hotel with less anxiety. She was now the sole owner and manager, her mother, Mary Saalmuller, having died late in 1936.

And so Wega Little continued to thrive in Brummana – Lebanese not by race but by birth. She had integrated herself into the culture and was much loved and respected by her neighbors. When she retired in 1954 and went to live with Stephana and Charles Armbruster in Majorca, she left the only home that she had ever known – the little village of Brummana set in the hills of the Lebanon overlooking the Mediterranean Sea.

Wega and Thomas Little

Bibliography (Part III)

1. Armbruster, Stephana. Life and History of John Bell and his Descendants. Palma de Mallorca: 1966.
2. Fox, Annie E. Thomas Little; or From Rawdon to Brummana. Friends Foreign Mission Association, London: 1916.
3. Turtle, Henry John. Quaker Service. Headly Brothers Ltd. London: 1975.
4. An unpublished diary of Stephana Armbruster.
5. An unpublished diary of Thomas Little

Part IV

Stalky and Ve

Wherefore praise we famous men
From whose bays we borrow -
They that put aside Today –
All the joy of their Today –
And with toil of their Today –
Bought for us tomorrow!
   —Rudyard Kipling

In Their Generations

Wega Miller George

They called each other Stalky and Ve: their real names were Theodore (Ted) and Vera. She must have read Kipling's rollicking tale of three sixth formers in an English prep school when she was growing up in Yorkshire. When she met Ted Miller in Cairo in 1924, she immediately harkened back to their leader, Stalky Corkran, a far-from-conventional hero who had an unerring gift for righting wrongs, outwitting classmates and masters alike and leading his cohorts on frequent and audacious exploits. He was her Stalky – the first, and only, love of her life. As the years went by she became his loyal "Co.", whom he dubbed Ve.

Theodore Evan Miller was an American, born in 1899, and raised in Bridgeton, New Jersey, on his father's produce farm. In later years he would say of this man that he knew no other with a greater affinity for the land. I remember Grandfather Miller with twinkling blue eyes and a winsome smile. My father's mother was from a dour Scots family – a kindly woman, but not given to demonstrations of affection. As a little boy he remembered himself as quite chubby, but as the years went by he grew tall, and inordinately handsome. He had his father's cornflower blue eyes, and his smile would light up everything around him. As a teenager he used to truck the farm's fruits and vegetables to Philadelphia and handle the sales for his father. After graduating with honors from the Bridgeton High School in 1916, he continued to work with his father for nearly a year and then, lying about his age, he joined the navy, fearing that the war in Europe would be over before he could serve. He never got any farther than the Boston naval yard; and during the Armistice Day parade he rode flat on his back in a government ambulance, overcome by a severe case of mumps. Upon his discharge from the Navy he returned to New Jersey and entered Lafayette College, majoring in English literature, but including a good smattering of math and science to his curriculum. He graduated in the spring of 1921.

From Lafayette he entered Princeton Theological Seminary as a junior. Sometime during that year he learned of openings for short term teaching positions at the American University at Cairo, Egypt. Submitting his application in a large, competitive field, he was hired to teach English and to begin work in the fall of 1922; but when he arrived at the school the position in the English department had mistakenly been filled. He taught Physics instead. It became the family joke, but he simply had an amazing mind. Being also modest, he insisted that he continually struggled to keep ahead of his class.

The three years in Egypt were happy ones. In letters home he talked about his surroundings, his work and the social life he shared with his fellow instructors. One letter described the local farming to his father, even to include a photograph of oxen yoked to a plow breaking clods of the heavy, black earth. He observed that, " ... [t]he typical native takes life as it comes, has always time to talk, loves an argument, and is usually content with the state in which he finds himself". Again he notes, "We had a holiday on Friday because the students were to have a demonstration showing their loyalty to the king. The government evidently either misinterpreted the demonstration or feared the consequences, for the soldiers and police broke up the parade and the demonstration fell flat." He also reported that the Egyptians seemed to hate the English, and all things English, believing that they were in the country for what they could get out of it. In contrast, they appeared to accept the Americans, persuaded that they had no financial or political game to play.

Teaching, as rigorous as it proved to be, did not occupy all of his time. He and his peers found opportunities for sailing on the Nile, desert hiking and camping trips, and social events with their compatriots. No American holiday was allowed to go by without recognition of some sort, and at Christmas the university group met at one of the professor's homes where a fireplace and candle-bedecked Christmas tree added greatly to the pleasure of the evening. It must have been at one such social occasion that he first met Vera Little.

She had come to Cairo to teach little children at an English school. Throughout her life, even well into her seventies, my mother was singularly absorbed by her profession and her love of teaching. Surely she had observed her father's devotion to the process of education – his delight in instruction must have entered her very pores – and she had chosen his passion as her own. Her school years in England mirrored his, with an apparent early predilection for teaching and a love of sports. Thomas Little had taught her a daunting game of tennis and to swim competently. In Darlington she was soon running up and down the hockey field, playing left wing for her school's team. She rounded out her skills in language, education and sports with a sufficient capability at the piano; and with her very real sense of fun and wonder, she was eminently qualified for the work she loved.

Sometime in the autumn of 1924, she and Ted Miller met at one of the University's faculty functions. He was tall and well-spoken, and he echoed her father's interest in missions and education. She was diminutive (a full head shorter than he), darkly pretty, and lively but very shy. Gravitating to each other, there were no lack of social occasions to nurture a romance. Imagine afternoons of tennis and then tea on an outdoor terrace, bicycle trips out to the desert, and dances under an African night sky. Inevitably, they went together to the Bazaar in Cairo to choose three diamonds for a very traditional engagement ring setting. Their wedding was set for the 18th of April in 1925. The date must have been chosen to coincide with their spring break. Vera had one stipulation. Knowing that Ted Miller planned to enter the ministry, she insisted that he always be the one in the family to do any public speaking. Outgoing and expressive in the company of young children, she was terrified of standing up in front of an adult audience.

Her sister wrote to their grandmother Mary Saalmuller, who remained at home in Brummana, about the wedding festivities. Her listing of wedding gifts included their mother's present of a lovely Georgian silver tea service and, from a Mr. Grosse, the ubiquitous set of twelve, silver apostle teaspoons with matching sugar tongs. Auntie Fana had sent silver salt and mustard pots with matching pepper shakers, and the children at her school presented the couple with a set of brass vases. Vera worked through the day before her wedding; but Sylvia, who was then employed at the Kitchener Memorial Hospital in Cairo, took that day off to run errands and arrange flowers. She wrote of baths full of white roses, asparagus fern and palm arches. When Vera got off work at 3:00 in the afternoon they had tea with their mother, and Sylvia tried on her maid-of-honor's dress – lace and net with a primrose lining. It was lovely.

The next morning they were up early to arrange more flowers and to set out the wedding buffet with little sandwiches, cakes, and sweets. Sylvia, herself, made up Vera's bouquet of white rosebuds and the palest pink carnations. The wedding dress was simply made of ivory and gold brocade with orange blossoms trailing down one side. Sylvia thought it quite chic with its ankle-length skirt and crepe georgette sleeves. The veil was of Brussels lace, and was held on to her head with a band of orange blossoms.

Vera and her mother, followed by Sylvia and Mr. Grosse (who would give the bride away) were driven in two closed "glass motors" to the minister's home where the wedding was to take place. Then there were Ted and his best man waiting for them in the drawing room. The sun shone through the large bay windows as Vera, on Mr. Grosse's arm, walked to join her darling Stalky.

Sylvia described the ceremony as beautiful and short, during which she proudly clutched her sister's bouquet and gloves. The only witnesses to the event, other than the wedding party and their mother, were the minister's mother and the American consul. It was followed by a generous reception of ices and cakes that threatened to spoil their appetites for the wedding breakfast to follow.

Ted and Vera honeymooned in Jerusalem, taking numerous excursions out into the Palestinian countryside. In later years, when Ted Miller would recall Christ's life to his congregations in Pittsburgh, Baltimore or Brooklyn; they could see the rocky, dusty countryside of Judea and Galilee through his eyes, feel the heat and breathe in the pungent odors of farm animals and winnowed grain. But for Stalky and Ve in the latter part of April, 1925, the wonder was in their new life together.

They returned to Cairo to complete their teaching obligations for the school year, and stayed on for a few extra weeks to explore together the ancient monuments of the country. In a postcard to her new in-laws, Vera spoke of visiting the Luxor Temple pylon and obelisk, and then sitting on a terrace overlooking the Nile and seeing the mountains beyond. Their days in Egypt were, for both of them, a time to harken back to and cherish all of their lives.

~

By late summer Ted and Vera left the near Eastern world they had both come to love and moved on to the University of Edinburgh. For Vera it meant leaving her much-loved family behind, but she had known when she married her American that that would inevitably happen. They would spend the next two years in Scotland so that Ted could complete his Masters in Divinity and build up some doctoral coursework. In spite of being in the heart of the Presbyterian church of his childhood, he had already made his decision to enter the ministry as a Baptist. His addiction to his own personal freedom dictated his separation from any hierarchical organization of the church. Vera was able to pursue her love of teaching little children, and in their second year Ted routinely preached at the Marshall Street Baptist Church in Edinburgh. In order to explore the surrounding countryside, they bought a second-hand Sunbeam motorbike with a sidecar. Ted described it as their "trusty steed", saying that it was not much to look at, but very dependable. Then they would both go into gales of laughter remembering the times when his acceleration of the engine left the sidecar motionless at the edge of the road, with Vera sitting helpless on its cushions.

These were happy days in Scotland. Their memories were so fond that forty years later, when Ted retired in 1967, they returned to Edinburgh to spend another year of study and travel. But in 1927, they were forced into a sort of rupture. In order to return to the United States to take up his life's work, Ted Miller had to leave Vera behind and precede her back home so as to establish residency for a year. It was not until this was accomplished that she would be permitted to follow him. They separated on the southern coast of England, he to sail to New York and then to travel on to the promise of a position in Pittsburgh, Pennsylvania; and she to return to her family's hotel in Brummana to wait for his summons.

~

She loved to tell me about her harrowing first day in New York City in the autumn of 1928. After their ecstatic reunion on a dock in southern Manhattan, Ted and Vera headed underground to take a subway to Grand Central Station. It was a weekday and the station was crowded. When their train pulled up to the platform, the crowd surged forward and Ted pushed Ve ahead of himself through the car door in front of them. Suddenly the door slammed shut and there she was, inside the train with Ted left standing on the platform. She was alone in a new country and quite unaware of where she was or where she should go; but she did have enough experience of travel to gather her wits, step off the train at the very next station, and stand still. In a few minutes the next train brought her much-shaken husband to her side. Now, holding tightly to each other, they proceeded to Grand Central and caught the train to their new home.

Ted had found employment at the First Baptist Church of Pittsburgh, located downtown at the corner of Bellefield Avenue and Bayard Street. He was working there as the Junior Minister under Dr. Wallace Petty, a man whom he came to esteem and love. Vera found a teaching position in a local private school. In their naivety they contracted to rent a little apartment that turned out to lack a kitchen sink, so Vera did the dishes in the bathtub. Among her many attributes she could not lay claim to domesticity.

In Pittsburgh there were new friends to cherish for a lifetime. Closest of all were Sam and Mary Ewart, whom my brother and I knew later as Uncle Sam and Mamie Tattie. The two couples shared the pleasures of reading clubs, local concerts and cozy dinners, and Sam and Mary seemed particularly to treasure the companionship of the bright, young minister and his ebullient British bride. And there was something else that drew the two young couples together in empathy; neither seemed to be able to have children. The lack was particularly difficult for Vera, who was professionally absorbed with the care and education of pre-schoolers. For Sam and Mary Ewart the answer was adoption, and so this new consideration began to take hold of Ted's and Vera's thinking. I believe that my father would have been quite content to continue their life together without the encumbrance of children. These were the years during the depression of the '30's and, although they were both employed, their income was modest. But he fully recognized his wife's absorption in the young and her yearning for children of their own, and he did not stand in the way of her exploration of this new option. Early in 1933, Ted Miller accepted the offer of a church of his own and assumed the position of minister of the First Baptist Church of Baltimore. It was located in the neighborhood of Forest Park, on Liberty Heights Avenue, and he and Vera moved into a first floor apartment in a brown shingled house on Maine Avenue close by. By September they had also become parents, adopting their first child, Charles Samuel Miller.

They named him for Vera's brother, Charles, and for their dear friend in Pittsburgh, Sam Ewart; but being unsure of her family's acceptance of an adopted child, they used his second name. To Vera, in his early years, he was always "Sammy, darling". Two and a half years later, when I joined them, and now sure of her family's joy in their adopted children, I was named for everyone in sight. My first name was Wega, for my maternal grandmother; and then there was Beatrice, for my paternal grandmother; and Marie, for my maternal great grandmother. I spent my early years explaining to anyone who would listen that in German, a 'W' is pronounced as a 'V'.

My first memory is of a green balloon. My mother and father had saved diligently and, by the spring of 1938, when I was two years old and my brother still just four, they had bought tickets for the lovely, new Italian ocean liner, the *Conte Di Savoia* (built at Sparrows Point in 1932). My mother and we two children were on our way to visit her family in Brummana. To Sam's great delight, the weather was unseasonably rough and his joy in the enormous oceanic waves was so great that he sat on the edge of his bunk and hollered, "God, please let the ship roll over, please roll it over", while mother and I were continually, desperately seasick. When we finally arrived safely in the Port of Naples, Auntie Fana came to the pier to meet us in an open carriage drawn by two beautiful horses. Sam was given a red balloon and I a green one that, in my toddler stubbornness, I refused to have tied to my buttonhole. Soon, to my dismay, I watched it drift upward and slowly out of sight.

My mother's reunion with her family in Brummana was a rapturous event for all. She had been away from them for eleven years, ever since Ted had established residency for her in Pittsburgh. Both Chas and Sylvia were on hand to greet her, and Wega Little was overjoyed. My brother still remembers the outlay of the family's hotel with its entrance into a central hallway that led directly back to a large dining room covering the entire rear of the building. A door in the left side of the hall led to Uncle Chas' family's apartment where our younger cousin, Christopher, was always ready to play. A door on the right opened into my grandmother's rooms and her office.

In the weeks that followed there were family teas, picnics, and long walks through the countryside. Auntie Sylvia would toss me up on her shoulders and take me along wherever she went. The plan was that we should stay for a year, but tensions were building in Europe and there began to be talk of German U-boats. Sam celebrated his fifth birthday at the hotel on the 1st of August, while in Baltimore our father was hastening to discover a way to bring us safely home. By the end of the month we had boarded the *Exochorda*, a ship of the American Export Line. It was a small vessel carrying freight, except for fifteen to twenty passengers, and was one of the last ships to cross the Atlantic before the German U-boats began to take their toll.

We quickly settled back into our family routine. My father had found us the first-floor apartment in a large, three-story house on Oakford Avenue. It enjoyed a spacious yard with two wonderfully climbable cherry trees and open fields beyond. Mother had decided that it was time for her to re-enter her profession and obtained a teaching position at the Friends school in Baltimore. Once again her father was influencing her career. We children were enrolled there; Sam in the kindergarten and I in the nursery school, and we three spent the next twelve school years at Baltimore Friends.

The following years were blissfully happy for two little children growing up. Sam began piano lessons with one, Richard Goodman, whose family had fortuitously left Europe a generation before. I joined him when I turned five. While never (either one of us) becoming accomplished, we had always loved the classical themes with which we were surrounded at home, and equally loved to visit Goodman's lovely four-story brick row house on Bolton Street, where the grand piano sat imposingly in the two tall front windows.

There was our Daddy, who would always have a lap to climb into when I had a book in my hands; and our Mother who, I am sure, never felt an obligation to entertain us but who could not, herself, resist playing. My mind recaptures an image of she and Sam chasing through the house and yard – she with a broom in her hands and both in gales of laughter. I would be sitting on the porch rail with a book, and while their hearty games were not my style, I reveled in their sheer joy.

We were in church every Sunday, and basked in the warm affection of those around us. Particularly delightful were the occasional church suppers when the women of German-American descent would cook delicious piles of sauerkraut to accompany turkey dinners with bowls of gravy and mounds of mashed potatoes.

On Sunday afternoons after church, we most often had dinner at May Dean's house. She was a teacher in the public school system who loved my parents' intelligent conversation and had time to cook and entertain. We would be joined by her elderly aunt and uncle, whom we all fondly knew as Mama and Papa Coe. After our meal Daddy and Papa Coe would go into the living room where they would enjoy the ritual of lighting and smoking their after-dinner cigars. One of them would always give me the gilded paper ring from the cigar wrapping. The women would tidy up the kitchen and Sam and I would pull games out of a well-known cupboard and wile away the afternoon with Tiddlywinks or Checkers. It was on one such Sunday late in 1941, when we had all finally left church and piled over to May Dean's house for a leisurely dinner, that Daddy turned on the old Philco radio in the sunroom and we were accosted by John Daly's familiar voice announcing the invasion of Pearl Harbor.

~

There were two great events in the middle of the twentieth century that shaped Ted's and Vera's lives, and they both rose to meet each one with courage and with grace. The first was the entrance of the United States into the Second World War: the second was to be the American Civil Rights Movement.

On the 7th of December, 1941, Ted Miller was 42 years old. He had a wife, two children and employment at a church that he loved and where he was well valued. Life was happy, busy and comfortable even though it was often a challenge to make ends meet; but as soon as his country was at war he enlisted. He very simply explained that whenever the war might be over he could never again work effectively as a pastor unless he served the next generation when they were at peril, and shared such horrors as they must come to know. He also had the luxury of certainty that his wife was absolutely capable of managing the family in his absence. To her credit, Vera never balked. She knew there was no valid argument against his, and that letting him go without debate would be her gift. For the second time in his life,

Ted Miller enlisted in the Navy.

Before we knew it we were all bundled into the family's Nash to visit my father's parents and his sister's family in New Jersey. There was the drive north from Baltimore on old Highway 40 through Maryland and Delaware until we reached the Delaware River at New Castle. Here, as usual, we stopped for lunch at the old town's refurbished Statehouse, and then drove the car up the ramp to board the New Castle Ferry. On the other side, at Penn's Grove in New Jersey, we bumped off the ferry ramp and drove on through the southern Jersey farmland to Bridgeton. As we rode along the old two-lane country roads, the telephone lines would dip and loop beside us – whoop, whoop, whoop; and Sam and I would eagerly look for the occasional series of small Burma Shave signs that would suddenly appear along the roadside:

"I've lost my heart
To you", said Fred
"Then lose those whiskers
NOW!" she said
BURMA SHAVE

When we reached our grandfather's farm, as always, there was a ride on Lady, the white plow horse; and there were caramel candies in the amber glass bowl in the living room. It was a time for sons all over America to say goodbye.

Our goodbye took place at Baltimore Harbor. In 1942, the harbor was not the showcase that it has come to be; but a busy, grimy wartime series of docks. Ted was scheduled to take the regular overnight steamer from Baltimore down the eastern coast to Norfolk, Virginia, where he was to undergo his initial training. I remember boarding the ship with him to clamber up and down narrow stairways to find his berth in a tiny stateroom. He was terribly handsome in his new naval uniform, and we were heartbroken. His parting words were all to cheer us. There still exists a letter from Ted to his sister, Minnie, written from the Chaplains' School at Norfolk dated September 2, 1942. He had learned that his existing life insurance would be void if his death occurred in an airplane, and had taken out additional insurance and named her a contingent beneficiary to care for his children if Vera should predecease him. He assured her that he did not expect to be killed, but wanted her "… to receive the money for Sammy and Wega …" if things did not go as he hoped.

After Norfolk he was sent to Quonset Point in Rhode Island and finally to Bainbridge in Maryland. Mother was able to drive us up to visit him there, and we had lunch in the officers' dining room where, as usual, I was reminded of the starving Armenians my grandmother had fed and compelled to eat the dandelion greens in my salad.

~

My brother does not remember, but it is one of the distinct recollections of my early years, that we nearly lost our father at the very outset of his time at sea. The first ship to which he had been ordered was sunk, with all hands, off the coast of North Africa. By some great good fortune Ted Miller had missed her departure and his orders had been changed to the *U. S. S. Anne Arundel*. She had originally been placed into service by the Moore-McCormack Line as the *S. S. Mormacyork* in early 1941. The Navy assumed her title the following year, renamed her, converted her into an armed troop transport and placed her into commission in September of 1942. (5, p. 3)

Her first assignment of the war was to participate as a troop and equipment transport in the American portion of the invasion of North Africa, beginning in November of 1942. The leaders of the Allied forces, prodded by Winston Churchill, had decided that their first objective in the European theater of the war in 1942 should be the occupation of the entire coastline of Africa and the Levant. (1, p. 648) The initial American effort was to be an invasion of the coastal area of Morocco with landings at Fedala (near Casablanca), Safi and Port Lyautey. The *Anne Arundel*, with my father on board, sailed from Norfolk for Port Lyautey and participated in this initial effort to dislodge the Vichy French. Fedala and Safi were soon accomplished, with those two towns falling to George Patton's forces in less than ten hours, but there was fierce fighting at Port Lyautey where a strategic airfield rendered resistance more obstinate. Some ships of the French fleet came out of the harbor to attack the American transport ships while they were disembarking troops and supplies into landing craft. This was Ted Miller's first experience of the enemy. Under cover of escorting American warships, the troops were safely landed and the few Vichy ships either sunk or beached. (2, p. 138)

In the months between the landing at Port Lyautey and the subsequent invasion at Gela, Sicily; the *Anne Arundel* plied back and forth between New York and Oran, Algeria, carrying men and equipment. There are photographs taken during this period in the ship's history book of services conducted on deck with the church pennant flying. During all of his time at sea Ted carried two very small books in his pocket – one, a government issued "Prayer Book for Soldiers and Sailors" and the other a miniature notebook of his own making containing both the marriage and the funeral services, a few poems and some pages with his own thoughts typed up:

Give especially to those who most intimately mourn his going, a wide margin of comfort around their spiritual need and deep wells from which to draw consolation.

And...

Once more we stand upon the shore and bid farewell to a ship that loses itself over the rim of the world. Oh God give fair voyaging and safe harbor! As we stand upon this hither shore and bid farewell, grant us faith to hear the voices which on yonder shore cry "Welcome!" and "All Hail!"

To those who suffered my father was able to lend comfort, encompassed by dignity and beauty.

At home we were adjusting to his absence. With strategic materials becoming rationed, we now seldom used the car. Tires and gas were only to be used when absolutely necessary, so we began to frequent the city's streetcars. Our school was at least fifteen miles from where we lived, so each morning the three of us would climb aboard the Number 31 streetcar that passed by at the top of Oakford Avenue. We would ride it all of the way to the car barn, where we would change to the Number 25. The delight of the next segment of our trip was to pass by the stables of Baltimore's famous Pamlico racetrack and watch the elegant horses enjoying their early morning exercise. Number 25 took us on to Falls Road at the bottom of Roland Park where we would clamber off at the intersection of Deep Dean Road and begin the mile long trek to reach Friends School. There was a low rock fence along one stretch of incline, and we children would delight to walk atop its uneven ridges. The last bit of our morning peregrination was along a seldom used railroad track and then across the stepping stones of a small stream. From here the school was just a playing field's distance away.

Her French cousins became our Mother's growing concern, and our out-grown clothes were carefully packed, along with chocolate and other scarce treats, to be sent to her Auntie Marilie's grandchildren in Montpellier in the south of France. And having grown up in England where knitting had become second nature to her, she was always working on a sweater or cap either for us or for one of the French cousins. How well I remember her utter frustration when she was called down by the Head Mistress of the Lower School for knitting during a faculty meeting. Her attention had never been diverted, and she had been making good use of her time.

One of the happy instances of those early war years was the gift of a dog from Richard Goodman, our piano teacher. He must have recognized Mother's nervousness with her husband so far away, and offered her one of his three wire-haired fox terriers to serve as a façade of protection. Sonny became our delightful companion for years to come.

As for my father's church, they were able to hire a young man straight from divinity school as their interim minister; but in the vestibule, at the left side of the entrance, they hung a beautifully framed photograph of Ted Miller in his navy blues and his officer's hat. We still had Sunday dinners at May Dean's house in the reassuring company of Mama and Papa Coe, but there was an emptiness in these routines and a vague restiveness in our lives.

~

After more than seven months of convoy duty, the *Anne Arundel* returned to amphibious warfare. This time the objective was the island of Sicily that lay between the coast of North Africa and the toe of the Italian boot. The idea was that the entire Mediterranean should be in Anglo-American hands to prepare for the liberation of Southern and Western Europe. (1, p. 656) In July of 1943, in an armada of landing forces, the *Anne Arundel* steamed toward the beaches at Gela, undergoing a severe German Stuka bombing attack. (5, p. 3) My father's duty station, both then and for the rest of his time aboard, was on the bridge rather than in the sick bay, as might have been expected. He told us later how much easier it was for him to be able to see what was coming at him than to feel entombed below deck. We know that by the end of August, the invasion of the island was a success, but not before 35,000 German soldiers had managed to escape across the narrow straights of Messina to Italy, to fight another day in the battles of Salerno, Cassino and Anzio. (4, p. 184) The *Anne Arundel* returned to convoy duty in the North Atlantic. Escorted by destroyers and other heavy warships she routinely sped between New York and the British Isles, carrying supplies and evading the German U-boats that menaced her every crossing.

At home we maintained our routines, including the family's annual vacation. Each summer since we had begun school, Mother had organized a family holiday – usually a trip to a state park to camp in a tent or a cabin for two weeks and enjoy swimming, boating and hiking. Even in the summer of 1942, our father had obtained leave to join us at a State Park in western Maryland. In 1943, my mother saw no reason to wallow in worry and every reason to continue family tradition. Her plan for us, somewhat ambitious, was to go cycling though some of the national historic sites in Pennsylvania. She collected information and maps from American Youth Hostels and organized an itinerary that would include visits to Philadelphia, Valley Forge and Gettysburg. That summer I was all of seven years old and Sam was not quite ten.

Early on a bright morning in July, she packed Sam and me into the blue Nash, along with our bikes and her light-weight English racer, and drove in town to the Mt. Vernon Station to catch the B & O to Philadelphia. Leaving the car in the station lot, we loaded our bikes into the end of one of the train carriages and, carrying our knapsacks, we climbed aboard. It was still morning when we arrived, and we were soon cycling northwest out of the city and along the Schuylkill River. It was grand!

Our destination that first day was Norristown, some twelve to thirteen miles away. Mother had been careful to choose only those routes that were described as mostly level. Usually Sam led the way, with me following and Mother assiduously herding us from behind. The countryside was lovely, with tidy farmland along the way, but as the afternoon wore on even the slightest incline became challenging and it was with much relief that we reached our first hostel – a barn on a local farm that had been only slightly renovated to accommodate overnight guests.

My fond memory of Norristown is a simple supper of homemade soup. Mother had chosen a local café for our evening meal. We were, by this time, so tired; and the chicken noodle soup with vegetables was everything that I wanted or needed. I chose it for desert as well.

We fell into bed that evening, barely brushing our teeth, so the next morning Mother insisted upon full ablutions. The shower rigged in the horse stall near our beds yielded the most frigid water that we had ever encountered. But the day was fresh and bright, and we were eager to pursue our prescribed route to Valley Forge.

We began well, again enjoying the surrounding sights, but as we progressed the road began to rise ever so slowly, without relief. I would be the first to falter and give in to walking my bike, and Mother would have to join me. Sometimes the road would level a little and we could remount our bikes, and then the incline would increase again. Our climb seemed interminable. At last, a couple of hours later, we crested a final rise and looked across the land and down into Valley Forge. We had made it. Sam and I leapt onto our bikes to indulge in the marvelous joy of a downhill run. There were soldiers parading in a field to the left and, absorbed in the delight of a marching band, I lost control of my bike and crashed into my brother. That was the end of our bicycle tour in Pennsylvania. A well-placed First Aide Station at the bottom of the hill came to our rescue. I was covered with cuts and bruises, but not seriously injured. Our hostel for that night was a comfortable cottage nearby, and I reveled in clean sheets and a soft mattress. The next day we were driven back to Philadelphia and boarded the train for home.

But the trip was not a disaster. In our minds it became woven into the fabric of a childhood filled with happiness and adventure. Ted Miller had known perfectly well when he left for the war that his Ve would keep the family moving forward and well-engaged with life.

~

In 1944 the Allies were preparing for the invasion of Normandy. In March, the *Anne Arundel* took on board a load of amphibious assault craft with their crews, along with other war material carried in her lower holds, and sailed for the British Isles. April and May were spent in rigorous training exercises. Just ten days before the landings on the coast of Normandy, the ship, along with others destined for the offensive at Omaha Beach, underwent "... an intensive low level bombing attack by the [German] Luftwaffe ...", but the *Anne Arundel* survived unscathed. (5, p. 3) The ship was loaded with invading troops on the 4th of June and, at 4:00 in the morning of the 5th, Eisenhower made his final decision to proceed with the invasion. (2, p. 630) All that day the ships that were to carry the spearhead of the invasion gathered off the coast of the Isle of Wight. My father saw the enormity of the assembled ships and marveled at its mass as far as the eye could see. He conducted services, comforted individuals and prayed with them all. He was where he had meant to be and a part of "... [a]n immense armada of upwards of 4,000 ships, together with several thousand smaller craft [that] crossed the Channel." (3, p. 5) This was why he had been gone from his family for nearly two years – to serve his fellows in this moment of history. On the morning of June 6, 1944 the *Anne Arundel* "... rolled in the long ground swells close by the cruiser *Augusta* off Omaha Beach...." (5, p. 3)

At Omaha, unlike at the other sections of the Normandy coast, the Allied losses were dreadful. Three thousand men fell there that day. It was here that Field Marshal Rommel had succeeded in building up effective coastal defenses. His guns and men, firing from high bluffs, made a shambles of the beachhead. (4, p. 261) Those on the *Anne Arundel* were aware of the devastation, and she shuttled back to England with a cargo of wounded. Ted Miller walked between the stretchers laid out on the deck, talking and comforting.

The ship's last assignment in Europe was to support a landing through the underbelly of the continent along the Riviera. "The morning of August 15, 1944, found *Anne Arundel* off the swank Riviera beaches at the Baie de Pampelonne where she unloaded crack units of the battle-seasoned 3rd and 45th Divisions." (5, p. 3) She remained as a support vessel in the Mediterranean until late in October.

Mother's plans for our summer of 1944 were physically less rigorous than those of the previous year. Of course we tended our Victory garden, as did so many in the country, but our travel would be to New York State. Our first stop was at the campus of Vassar College in Poughkeepsie. She had enrolled herself in a workshop for teachers wanting to hone professional skills and to enjoy a creative boost in their artistic and intellectual activity. We children participated in an associated summer camp. At the end of the week the three of us piled into the car and drove on to Lake George.

That was one of the summers in this country when polio was rampant, and as we drove through the day, Sam became quiet and his temperature began to rise. By the time we reached Jerry Grusner's rental business for camping equipment at Bolton Landing on the east shore of the lake, my brother was quite sick and I was thoroughly frightened. I know my Mother was uneasy, but she filled Sam with fluids and the kind owner of the rental business allowed us to spend the night in his warehouse. By the next morning Sam was improving. We were entertained by Jerry Grusner's handsome Doberman, who, bowing his head, would say grace before his meals and would not eat until Jerry had pronounced "Amen". Too, we were enthralled by the fragrance and beauty of the well-forested lake shore. As we were novice canoers, a power boat carried us out to our island campsite, but then we were on our own to erect our tent and settle in. A fellow camper on an adjacent island noticed our ineptitude and paddled over to help.

It was a wonderful week. We swam and canoed and explored our island. At that time Lake George was so clean and clear that we were instructed to use its water to drink. Our family joke was Sam, who after swimming for awhile rushed out of the lake to ask for a drink of water. All too soon we returned to shore to return our camping equipment and bid farewell to Jerry and his dog. We had added another splendid vacation to tuck into our family memory.

Late in the autumn of 1944 our father came home on leave. The *Anne Arundel* had come from the Mediterranean for sorely needed repair and overhauling to ready her for the war in the Pacific. It was sheer joy to have him with us once more, but our delight was tempered by the knowledge that he would soon be leaving for a different theatre. At that time there was a vague, but very real, perception that when fighting in Europe one had a reasonable chance of returning home, but that when sent to the Pacific one's chances decreased exponentially. It was so very hard to let him go again. The *Anne Arundel* sailed from New York City just a week before Christmas.

In Their Generations

~

For Ted Miller the *Anne Arundel's* passage through the Panama Canal was an unexpected delight during the difficult years of the war, and certainly a memorable experience in his life. The complete crossing of the isthmus took about twelve hours and most of the trip took place in silence through a largely undisturbed wilderness. "… [F]or those on board a ship in transit the effect of the greater part of the journey was sailing a magnificent lake in undiscovered country." (6, p. 614) The lake was spacious and its water was the green of the ocean. The sight of another ship appearing suddenly from around a bend ahead was quite startling, as one felt as if in an area untraveled and remote. Even the locks were relatively quiet. It was one of the world's wonders that he experienced and loved to recount to us.

From January through April of 1945, his ship carried troops and supplies to forward areas of fighting in the Pacific, and on return trips would evacuate the wounded from the island battles. Between May 3rd and May 9th, the *Anne Arundel* lay off the beaches of the western coast of Okinawa, unloading elements of the 10th Army. (5, p. 1) It was here that my father first witnessed the terrifying Kamikaze attacks on the American fleet. Okinawa might be described as the Pacific's epic amphibious operation, and it was finally secured on the 21st of June, but by that time my father was on his way home. The U. S. Navy knew that they were in the ascendancy, they were amply supplied with men and material, and they were now able to let a three-year veteran return to his home.

I had had two recurrent dreams during the years of the war. One was of that Philco radio at May Dean's house, shaped like a tombstone, announcing my death: the other was of my father driving down Oakford Avenue, returning home. It was the second dream that came true, while the first gradually faded from my psyche.

That summer Mother had delayed our family vacation until August, so that Dad could be with us. We continued our tradition of camping, but our 1945 holiday would be spent in the relative comfort of a log cabin. We all climbed into the old blue Nash, including Sonny, the dog, (who had an unfortunate propensity for motion sickness), and drove to Black Moshannon State Park, perched on the Allegheny plateau in Pennsylvania. In spite of our joy in being reunited, I remember that August in somber terms. Even the water of the lake, bubbling from fresh springs, was tinged the color of plants in the bog through which it flowed. My father spent hours with me to help me improve my swimming strokes, and even more time with his son who, of the three of us at home, had most resented his absence. Toward the end of the week a young boy drowned in the lake.

On the day that General MacArthur signed the peace treaty with the Japanese, my father sat by the maroon and silver portable Stromberg Carlson set on our picnic table, listening intently to the report of the ceremony. His face was a picture of concentration. Just as the ceremony ended we heard a sudden clap of thunder nearby. Our father looked up and smiled. The dreadful war was now behind us. He had done his part.

~

The next five years were a restless period in my parents' lives. For one thing, we moved four times. I had spent my entire nine years at Oakford Avenue, but now my parents decided to make their first purchase of a house. After the seven years that we had traveled miles to school every day, they bought a house in Roland Park from which we could easily walk. This meant that our father would have a long trip to the church, but gas was once more plentiful, and he needed the car anyway for meetings and pastoral calls. I think that Mother never liked the house. It was an older structure, made entirely of wood, and she always saw it as a fire hazard. By 1948, Ted and Vera were building a little brick house out in Pikesville – affordable, but convenient to nothing. We were to move in by early June, but the builder kept delaying. Finally he absolutely promised completion upon our return from yet another camping trip. When we showed up and the house was still not ready, Mother made her displeasure utterly clear by camping out in the back yard. We moved in within three days. It was only a few months after this clash of wills that the church acquired a pleasant house in its neighborhood and offered it to us as a parsonage. We moved again.

During this same time period, the head mistress of the lower school at Friends decided that Mother was too old to work with very little children and moved her, initially to teach the first grade and, subsequently, the third. This was the same woman who had chided her for knitting during a faculty meeting. She knew Vera Miller's reputation for excellence among both her peers and the large body of parents who, over the years, had come to value her prowess in the instruction of their children. Her seemingly arbitrary dictates were difficult for my mother to bend to.

In 1949, Mama Coe died. Mother never allowed us children to attend funerals, but we learned that just before her coffin was closed, Papa Coe threw himself over her body and wept uncontrollably. The Coes had been like surrogate parents to Ted and Vera, and grandparents to us, and we grieved with him. Life was beginning to change, and we were having to grow up.

These changes did not disturb the core solidity of our lives for Sam or for me. We continued at the only school that we had ever known, with our mother nearby and our father back in his pre-war position. But life was now different for both of them, and I think that they were ready when the pulpit committee from the Emmanuel Baptist Church of Brooklyn, New York, appeared in a pew at the First Baptist Church of Baltimore, on a Sunday morning in the spring of 1950.

~

There they were - Judge Orrin Judd with his wife, Persis, along with the McCanns (Joe and Lydia), Ed and Ethel Harriot, and Irving Nutt. The Emmanuel Baptist Church in Brooklyn had roots going back to the First Williamsburg Church founded in 1839. Over the years it had combined with other congregations and now, in 1950, it was beginning to welcome into its membership a group of people from Jamaica and one from Barbados who had moved into the neighborhood. Their minister was retiring and they were looking for someone who had the grace and fortitude to help them to continue the process of integrating their church. How they had learned of Ted Miller in Maryland, I do not know, but they had found their man.

My Father had been in Baltimore for seventeen years, had participated in many of the most consequential battles of the Second World War, and was now just fifty-one years old. He was more than ready for a new challenge. The visitors from Emmanuel Baptist heard a moving and articulate sermon that morning, preached by a minister at the height of his capabilities. There was no question of his qualification. Convinced that he was a man well-suited to their need, they offered him a handsome increase in his salary and the promise of a parsonage, to be purchased. He would spend the next seventeen years in Brooklyn.

That August, when we moved to Brooklyn, Sam was a rising senior at Friends, and a member of the school's lacrosse team. It was a terrible time for him to leave. Both he and I had been a part of the school's community for twelve years – he since kindergarten and I since nursery school. It was all that we knew. But Stalky's Ve went into overdrive. Our move, in her hands, became yet another adventure. She had long felt that my brother needed the firm guidance of an all male school. Adhering to her loyalty to private institutions, she found Sam a boys' preparatory school located in the area of Brooklyn known as the Narrows. Following her lead, and refusing to feel sorry for himself, he improved his grades and starred on their lacrosse team. Although there was a Friends School in Brooklyn, Mother chose, instead, to send me to a lovely girls' school on Joralemon Street in the Heights. And in her infinite kindness, when moving day arrived she packed May Dean into the car with us so that she could be a part of our transition, at least for a little while. I can remember that through all of the years that he was with us, my Father would say to me, "your Mother is a remarkable woman." Indeed, she was.

The parsonage that the church had bought was on the corner of Lafayette and Clermont Avenues and was an easy five block walk down Lafayette Avenue to the church. It had been constructed, years ago, as a "spite" house. The builder had wanted to give his daughter an impressive house as a wedding gift, but he had been thwarted in his attempt to buy an extensive amount of land at the chosen site. In reprisal, he had built the structure taller and longer than any other house on the block. It was really quite lovely, four stories high and constructed of a dark red brick. Mother had the fun of choosing new paint and wallpaper and spent the first weeks, with May Dean, sewing white cotton curtains for all of the many windows, adding a feeling of airiness and light. (They were dreadful to wash and iron.) When it was time for the fall semester of the school year to begin, May Dean sadly boarded the train back to Baltimore.

Ted Miller had stipulated that his new salary should be sufficient to enable his Ve to stay at home, and she did – for a while. She threw herself into supporting his position; entertaining church groups, teaching Sunday School, and beginning the tradition of an elaborate "at home" at the parsonage on the Sunday afternoon before Christmas. Right after Thanksgiving she would ease me into the kitchen and we would begin to bake, and we didn't stop baking and cooking until the day of the annual Christmas entertainment. She would be a whirlwind of activity, and I would scrub pans and clean up after her. Two or three days before the event she would initiate a frenzy of silver polishing – the tea service from her Mother, the silver candlesticks from the church in Pittsburgh and all the various serving utensils that she would use. It was an event that everyone looked forward to, even she and I. She had an uncanny ability to love the unlovely and make them feel wanted, and she was skillfully adept at diverting those who selfishly monopolized my father's time by beguiling them with the alternative attraction of her friendship. The one thing that she didn't do, and had never done, was to take communion in Ted Miller's church. In this, her Quaker upbringing prevailed, but her refusal was so quiet and unassuming, that no one took notice.

    As for me, my first day of school turned out to be a half day. With a delicious autumn afternoon stretching ahead, some of my new friends decided to go out to Ebbets Field to see the Dodgers play and begged me to come along. I saw the famed Jackie Robinson that day, along with Roy Campanella, PeeWee Reese and Gil Hodges. What better way to be welcomed to my new home town.

~

With his family happily and productively settled, my father was free to take up his new calling. Perhaps it was not entirely coincidental that the Emmanuel Baptist Church had identified Ted Miller to serve their need. In Baltimore, particularly after the war, he had worked diligently in ecumenical areas, and had completed his time there heading up the local Council of

Christians and Jews. This was no small task in a city bordering the conservatism of southern states, but he brought to the job eclectic skills and an irresistible enthusiasm for inclusiveness. The goal now was to warmly welcome any who crossed the threshold of the soaring stone edifice of Emmanuel and to hold, with bonds of steel, all those who were already there. It was not sufficient to be welcoming – he had to continually hold on to the old guard of staid Brooklyn families. His old skills lent themselves to his new task.

I think that Ted Miller had two forces at work within himself to meet the challenge. We had sometimes wondered how his impressive intellect could hold a southern congregation attuned to a simple, basic faith. In Brooklyn he could give full vent to the expression of the breadth of his learning. The original core of the church enjoyed a high level of educational achievement and responded eagerly to the challenge of his teaching. The new entrants were drawn by the warmth of his expression and the clarity of his message that brought comfort and hope. All were regaled with frequent reminders of their social responsibility to each other. I remember one sermon after another espousing the thrust of the message of the Apostle Paul, and his exhortations to the early church to care for one another. Sometimes I was afraid that the congregation would tire of my father's continuing reliance on the saint, but they never seemed to. It is also my clear recollection that somehow, (I was too young to understand why) my father's work drew the attention of Senator Joe McCarthy's Committee on un-American Activities, and he was blacklisted. It made no difference – my father knew that what he was about was unquestionably right.

Of course the third force at work for Ted Miller was his Ve. Her quiet warmth and generosity were always there to beguile the ambiguous or uncertain. Together they spent seventeen years, the remainder of his ministry, working at Emmanuel.

The church edifice had been completed in 1887 and was

impressive. Entering one of the three double doors in the soaring stone face, one was treated to an expansive interior that dazzled the senses with a vaulted roof, stenciled walls and rich, stained glass windows. I remember being told that the wooden ceiling was made of the same wood that is used to construct stringed instruments. Indeed, the acoustics were wonderful, and there was a pipe organ well able to exploit this setting. Most of the church members lived nearby in what is known as the Clinton Hill area of Brooklyn. On the corner across the street was the Adelphi Academy and two blocks behind was the Pratt Institute, well known for the excellence of its instruction in art and design. Emmanuel Baptist served people associated with both schools.

The congregation was replete with distinctive characters to engage our curiosity and affection. Perhaps the most memorable was the custodian, George Hooper. A native of Jamaica, he was a man grizzled with years and laden with wisdom. How many times did he pose questions to Sam or to me and challenge us to careful thought. Then on Easter mornings he would inevitably confront us with the old Anglican affirmation that "Christ is risen", and look expectantly at us. We, being ignorant of most things liturgical, would have to be coached to respond properly that "the Lord is risen indeed". It was not too many months before my father began to include the lovely general confession and thanksgiving from the Morning Prayer section of the "1928 Book of Common Prayer" in his Sunday morning service. George Hooper must have had his effect on Ted Miller as well as his children.

Then there were the Judds, with their four young children. Orrin was a distinguished jurist in Manhattan. He and his wife, Persis, had planned to name their intended offspring Pi, Ro, Tech and Nic, affirming their anticipated brilliance. The third child turned out to be a girl and was named Betsy, disrupting their scheme. The eldest, Pi, was my age and, some years later, served as an attendant at my wedding.

In Their Generations

Mr. and Mrs. Beecher Jackson had been one of the early black couples to join the church, and their daughter, Frances, was the first black child to have been baptized there. When we knew her, Frances Jackson was a tall, willowy young woman with a warm smile and a deep, chortling laugh who taught in the public school system. She became a dear friend.

Ed and Ethel Harriot, who were both leaders in the church, came to be my parents' close friends. Their charm was in their deep affection for each other. Ed usually referred to his wife as "Eddie" as if, indeed, she were the other part of himself.

After the first year in Brooklyn my mother went back to teaching. Sam had left for college, and there simply were not enough activities in the day to fully engage her. True to her training and experience she approached the Friends School in Brooklyn, and was given charge of their first grade. She continued there until she and my father retired in 1967.

The years in Brooklyn were useful and creative ones for both Ted and Vera. How well I remember my mother bending over her school projects that would be scattered across our large dining room table, while my father retired to his study to smoke a pipe, read prodigiously and write his sermons. I remember family meals – always at that well-polished table, and always with my father sitting at the head, pouring copious cups of tea for anyone present. On Saturday afternoons, broadcasts from the Metropolitan Opera would echo from his radio and from hers. On Sunday afternoons there would be a profound sense of restfulness in the house, and then a late tea that was both supper and a small boost into the coming week. My mother served a generation of young children and their grateful parents: my father succeeded in his mission to hold a church together and to serve its community.

Wega Miller George

~

The year that they retired, Ted and Vera packed their household goods into storage and set off for Edinburgh, Scotland, to recapture their early years of study and companionship. Eventually, they retired to Reston, Virginia, which they judged to be approximately halfway between Sam's household in Massachusetts and mine in North Carolina. We all loved to visit them there to soak in their love and their wisdom. Once again we would sit around that dining room table, reminisce and drink endless cups of tea. In 1983, when their health was beginning to fail, they came to live with me. My father died the following year and my mother began to enter the terrible abyss of dementia. Not long after his death I noticed her sitting in her chair, writing assiduously. Later, when she had left the piece of paper negligently behind, I glanced at its contents. "I see your face in the table," she had begun. I could read no more.

Bibliography (Part IV)

1. Churchill, Winston S., <u>The Grand Alliance</u>. Houghton Mifflin Co., Boston: 1951.
2. Churchill, Winston S., <u>Closing the Ring</u>. Houghton Mifflin Co., Boston: 1951.
3. Churchill, Winston S., <u>The Tide of Victory</u>. Houghton Mifflin Co., Boston: 1951.
4. <u>Life's Picture History of World War II</u>. Time Incorporated, New York: 1950.
5. Unpublished family letters.
6. <u>P76</u>. A pictorial history of the *U. S. S. Anne Arundel* published at the end of World War II for the members of her crew.
7. McCullough, David, <u>The Path Between the Seas</u>. Simon and Schuster, New York: 1977.

In Their Generations

EPILOGUE

In 1952, when I was sixteen, my mother returned from one of her routine trips to Majorca where she had been visiting her mother and Auntie Fana. Often, when she came back from these trips, she brought small family mementoes or souvenirs from the island; but this time she was carrying a woman's gold signet ring. It bore an image of the Lion of Judah, carrying a cross and wearing a beehive crown – the iconic representation of the Royal House of Ethiopia. Auntie Fana had sent it to me: I have worn it ever since.

Many years later I began to research my mother's family and, fortunately for me, there is a great deal to read. I traced the details of John Bell's amazing adventures. I discovered that his wife was the daughter of King Theodore's niece. I learned that we were not truly related to Peter Ustinov, but that we were bound to him through the unique company of the shared inheritance of Theodore's "Gaffat Children". Ustinov's forebear was Moritz Hall, who helped Waldmeier and Saalmuller to build the cannon, Sebastopol.

Finally, I traveled to Ethiopia to see this ancient land for myself. It is so rich in history and so very poor. It is extraordinarily diverse in its geographic features and very beautiful. The lions no longer roar in the night near Korata, but the little tanquas made of papyrus reeds still ply the waters of Lake Tana, and you can still see a hippopotomus swimming off the shore of the Zege peninsula. The people I met were welcoming and kind. I know why John Bell stayed.

I have learned to love the family that my mother so generously shared with me. While my own life can never match theirs for adventure or accomplishment; I have, at least, told their story.

Acknowledgments

I wish to express my deepest gratitude to my daughters, Kathy and Taela, who have read numerous drafts of the book and cheered me on from the very first page; to the staff of the Kill Devil Hills library in Dare County, North Carolina, especially Naomi Rhodes, who is a diligent researcher; and to Dr. Richard Pankhurst, the eminent historian of Ethiopia, who read an early draft and encouraged me to persevere.

My inspiration has always been the story, itself; and my mother, who told it with such pride.